The Professional Secretary's Handbook

COMMUNICATION SKILLS

John Spencer and Adrian Pruss

First edition for the United States and Canada
published 1997 by Barron's Educational Series, Inc.

First published in Great Britain under the title
The Professional Secretary Volume 1.

© 1995 by John Spencer and Adrian Pruss

By arrangement with Cassel plc
Wellington House, 125 Strand
London WC2R, 0BB, England

All inquiries should be addressed to:
Barron's Educational Series, Inc.
250 Wireless Boulevard
Hauppauge, New York 11788

Library of Congress Catalog Card No. 96-41843
International Standard Book No. 0-7641-0023-8

Library of Congress Cataloging-in-Publication Data
Spencer, John (John Leslie), 1954–
    [Professional secretary. v. 1. Communication skills]
    The professional secretary's handbook.   Communication skills /
John Spencer and Adrian Pruss.
       p.   cm.
    Originally published as vol. 1 of: The professional secretary /
John Spencer and Adrian Pruss. London : New York : Cassell, c1995.
    Includes index.
    ISBN 0-7641-0023-8
    1. Secretaries.   2. Office practice.   I. Pruss, Adrian.
    II. Title.
HF5547.5.S7242   1997
651.3'74—dc20   96-41843
                                                     CIP

PRINTED IN THE UNITED STATES OF AMERICA

987654321

Contents

Duties of the Reader   127

How to Write Large Documents, Such as Reports   127
    Only start drafting when you have the overall purpose   127
    Advantages of keeping the overall purpose in mind   128
    Disadvantages of having the big picture in mind throughout   128
    Think it out in advance   128
    Your writing will be appreciated through the eyes only   129
    Techniques of persuasion   129
    The next step   131
    The order of writing (which is not the order of presentation)   131
    Physical appearance of your report   131

Personal Presentations to Assist Reports   133
    How to make sure that your presentation is effective   135
    Advantages of personal presentations   136

Part 4 **Assertiveness**
        Belief–Behavior Feedback Loop   141

        What Are Your Rights?   144

        Outcomes of Assertiveness   146

        Characteristics of Behavior Patterns   147
            Passive nonassertion   147
            Dismissive nonassertion   148
            Aggression   148
            Assertion   149

        Types of Assertion   149
            Basic assertion   149
            Questioning assertion   149
            Empathetic assertion   150
            Discrepancy assertion   151
            Negative feelings assertion   152
            Outcome assertion   152

        Understanding Aggressive Behavior   153
            Why people become aggressive   153

        The Effects of Aggression   155
            The immediate responses generated   156
            Accumulated results of aggression   156
            Why you become nonassertive   158

Foreword

When I was editor of *Office Secretary* magazine, the largest circulation business journal for secretaries in the United Kingdom, two things always bothered me about the secretarial profession. One was the attitude that so many in the business world chose to adopt—that of undervaluing the secretary. The second was the sheer lack of corporate understanding that secretaries need proper business and management training, just like other office personnel, in order to improve their skills and enhance their value to an organization.

In my research I was sadly disappointed to learn that several U.K. companies, many of them large and impressive, had no provision whatsoever for further personal development and business training for their secretaries. They frequently resorted to an old cop-out: "We only ever take on fully qualified staff who have taken secretarial courses at college." Granted, but forgive my cynicism: I've never seen a management school graduate become managing director straight out of school. Instead, these people have all the benefits of structured training programs to get them there, do they not?

So why not a continuing program of training for secretaries?

There are two things that turn a good secretary into an excellent secretary: learning through experience at work and additional business training. That is why I searched for a solution to the dual problem that secretaries, my readers, were bringing to my attention: they wanted better recognition and prospects within their corporate environments, and not to be brushed aside as "just the secretary." And they wanted to gain a more creative role in management by acquiring new skills and improving old ones.

In my search for an answer, I discovered John Spencer, the co-author of this remarkable book. And he is rather a "discovery." We teamed up to design a specialized secretarial training program, focusing on both personal development in business and management training, which we could run in conjunction with *Office Secretary* magazine. Because of his fine-tuned ability to create a series of relevant, informative, and exciting courses, and to present them to delegates with humor, high impact, and empathy, our courses were a tremendous success.

This book is the offspring of these courses, together with the input of co-author Adrian Pruss. In it the Spencer-Pruss team conveys practical, relevant information for a secretary's everyday role. There is no unusable, "great on paper but not in reality," management theory. The charismatic and dynamic Spencer and Pruss, both of whom are knowledgeable and flexible presenters, understand the secretary's problems and opportunities. And they make learning fun!

This book captures in words what Spencer and Pruss do live. It is a performance on pages: of fascinating, refreshing information and ideas, guidelines to particular tasks, and key management ideas that can help the secretary's job to run more smoothly; all in a highly readable style. How will it help you?

This first of two books concentrates on communications. No secretary can do a professional job without being a good communicator, which is why this book explores in detail the essence of good telephone techniques, how to cope in meetings as an active member of the meeting, not a silent accessory, effective business writing (getting the message across in everything from memos to reports), and that one major problem area for so many secretaries: being assertive *enough* for the job.

Overall this book will help you learn and understand how you can expand your role in your organization, and how to improve your status in doing so, thereby protecting your job and your value to the company. You will be shown solutions to common secretarial problems and practical new ideas. This book will serve as both tutor and guide.

John and Adrian's skills as dynamic presenters, and as authors of several books between them, guarantee a lively and informative read. There won't be a dull moment.

Onay Faiz
Former Editor and Training Coordinator, *Office Secretary*
Currently Training Development Manager, The Training Network

About the Authors

John Spencer

Specialist trainer and lecturer in management development skills; specialist lecturer in accountancy, finance, and taxation. Consultant, lecturer, and trainer to the financial services sector. Organized, developed, and delivered the "Executive Secretaries into Management" training courses for delegates from over 200 leading companies. As well as industrial and commercial experience, he is retained by clients in the entertainment and media industries. Well-known contributor to magazine, radio, and TV media on a variety of "personal development" subjects. Author of many business books, and co-author with Adrian Pruss of *Managing Your Team* and *How to Implement Change in Your Company*.

Adrian Pruss

City-trained accountant. Prior to founding APW Training, positions held included academic and boardroom appointments. Now a management consultant specializing in organizational review, cost reduction, and change programs. A management development consultant and trainer for multinational, industrial, and commercial organizations in Europe, the United States, and Africa. Co-author with John Spencer of the books *Managing Your Team* and *How to Implement Change in Your Company*.

About APW Training

APW Training, the company run by John Spencer and Adrian Pruss, is at the fore-front of training that brings management level skills and approaches to secretarial development. Over the past four years, APW Training has delivered its courses to secretaries from over 200 leading companies worldwide.

Introduction

The secretary's success books contain the core skills needed by any secretary seeking promotion or a move into management. The skills outlined represent the most demanded courses in training programs run by the authors over 15 years. In the past four years, we have been delivering these courses to secretaries from over 200 of the top U.K. and international companies. The courses have addressed the real-world problems and issues of the modern secretary. Exit reports from those courses have been 100 percent positive. Typical comments made have been:

Dealt with the subject of time management in a straightforward and realistic way.

Course trainer was very good—he obviously understood the problems of meetings.

This was a constructive, positive course.

Excellent value, comfortable but speedy pace.

Very interesting and informative.

A good day with plenty of ideas to take back to the office.

The course was of a very high standard.

Never a dull moment. Interest maintained at all times.

Most enjoyable, entertaining, but most of all interesting and enormous help to progression in the 1990s.

An excellent day. I gained a great deal of knowledge.

Further feedback from delegates on the courses has indicated that they are able to use the material for career progress, job enhancement, and improving relationships with their bosses and others.

The training objectives of the courses, which are reflected in these books, meet the varied needs of secretaries who want to:

- make more of their jobs;
- acquire skills that will take them into executive secretary/administrative assistant standard;
- break the "glass ceiling" and move into management.

The Professional Secretary comes in two volumes:

Volume 1: Communication Skills covers:

- the most successful skills for meetings, minutes, and agendas;
- the most successful skills for using the telephone;
- the most successful skills for persuasive writing;
- the most successful assertiveness program.

Volume 2: Management Skills covers:

- the most successful skills of team management;
- the most successful skills of time management;
- the most successful skills of solo management;
- the most successful skills of motivation, influencing, and communication.

By following the very practical guidance in these two volumes, you will enhance your work, gain greater enjoyment from your work, and increase your chances of promotion ahead of less skilled colleagues.

Enjoy the books, enjoy your future work, and enjoy the promotion that will soon be coming your way.

PART 1

Meetings,
Agendas, and Minutes

The single greatest cause of dissatisfaction in modern corporate life in which secretaries are involved is probably to be found in meetings—an area in which a secretary, using the knowledge in this part of the book, can make enormous savings.

From direct feedback from several of our major U.K. clients, we know that the application of our training relating to the conduct of, chairing, and being secretary to meetings is saving thousands of staff hours per year. In addition, the time people spend in meetings is increasingly productive, active, and—usually an unheard of phrase for meetings!—enjoyable.

In this part of the book, you will discover practical and usable improvements that can be made in several areas of meetings administration. You will be able to make sure that meetings are set up with the best possible chance of success, involving the preparation of an effective agenda, very powerful techniques for minute taking, and a radical and highly practical way of publishing minutes.

With regard to *agenda setting*, the agenda style that we have taught to secretaries of over 150 major companies has resulted in entirely positive feedback. Our style of publishing minutes has an extraordinary goal that we have nonetheless been able to implement successfully; that no matter how long a set of minutes (even if they run to 20, 30, or 40 pages or more), those minutes should be designed to be read in no more than 30 seconds!

What Is a Meeting?

The word *meeting* could imply all kinds of coming together of people in all sorts of situations: accidentally meeting on the train, meeting in each other's offices, talking on the telephone, and so on. For the purpose of this section, we consider the meeting to be akin to the classic board meeting structure; a group of eight to twelve people seated around a table discussing a preplanned list of items. The discussions are designed to achieve certain purposes. There is also some formality to the proceedings in the sense that an official record will be maintained and almost certainly some actions will be authorized. Making those basic components come together in a highly effective way is the purpose of this section.

Why Have Meetings at All?

Many processes happen in meetings, but the major benefits can be summarized in two words: communication and learning. Meetings are held for the following reasons.

- To solve problems. The organization's most complex difficulties probably involve several different departments, and require input from a variety of experts and disciplines. The meeting is a forum for that level of problem solving.
- Decision making. There comes a time when an authorized body—perhaps the Board of Directors or some committee—has to come together and summarize its options and make a decision that will commit the company for the future.
- Postmortems. The wisest organizations have learned that the greatest advances can be made by learning from mistakes. Situations that have led to great success or great difficulty or failure should be analyzed in detail so that future successes can be designed and developed.
- Creating ideas. In order to keep progressing in a dynamic world and to stay ahead of competition, companies must recognize the need to develop new products, new services, and new presentations. Meetings are a good forum for creative people to put forward their views and ideas, where they can be examined in a constructively critical light. A good meeting will allow for visionary thinkers and pragmatic practical doers to come together so that they can make new workable ideas from creative thinking.
- Giving information. Some meetings require less interaction than others and a meetings format can be used for one person to convey information to others. In order for this not to be inappropriate—or indeed a complete waste of time— there are certain rules relating to this kind of meeting, which is known as a *briefing* meeting. We will come to these shortly.
- Progress reports. Some meetings are held regularly in order to update team or committee members on the progress of particular work. In particular, a project may have regular project meetings so that the whole team is aware of how individual sections of the work are progressing.
- Meetings that comply with legal or company requirements, e.g., health and safety. All companies must make sure that their staff are well briefed on health and safety matters. In some companies, where there are higher health and safety risks, this is a vitally important use of meetings. Health and safety meetings are generally a combination of briefing meetings and some interactive discussion.

All of the above, and other specialist functions, can be summarized under the heading of *communication*. One of the criteria for effective meetings is therefore that the administration of the meeting should encourage effective communication. We will be looking at the layout of the room, other details, the attitudes of the team around the table, and the various and very important secretarial functions you must be familiar with.

The second important product of meetings is learning. There are two forms of learning that go on in meetings: the overt and the covert.

Overt learning is what the people around the table learn about the work of other departments and other people; about the progress, or lack of it, that their company is making in certain areas; about the way employees in the company view the company; about the way the world views the company from outside; and so on.

In addition there is *covert learning*: the people around the table, whether they are conscious of it or not, are learning about each other. They are learning about how people negotiate with others; how they perform in a team; and how effective they are in presentation. They learn about each other's strengths and weaknesses. Subordinates learn something about the character of their bosses and vice versa. It is not unfair to say that good performance in a meeting is a plus mark on the career path. Bad performance in a meeting can certainly lead to promotion being blocked or to one's being passed over by someone whose interpersonal skills are more effective. At the extreme, if you are sent to a meeting to represent your boss, then how you perform is highly likely to affect his view of your promotion prospects.

The meeting must therefore be designed to produce the most effective forum for communication and learning. Within that, the various players—including you—must encourage open discussion, creative thinking, and the full involvement of all participants.

Team Building

There is a third reason for meetings, which is extremely important and should not be ignored when one is discussing the cost-effectiveness of meetings, or the use of alternatives to meetings. Some organizations have their key personnel all around the world and they are rarely able to get together and share experiences, ideas, and so on. Meetings can be a very effective form of *team building*—of bringing the team together and reinforcing its cohesion. If you determine that there is a need for this form of team building, then it may well be that you will bring people together when there may be other cost-effective alternatives for communication or learning.

If you do call a meeting for a team building purpose, then bear in mind that this is one of your desired outcomes. Make sure that you have thought about some processes or arrangements that will enhance team building. Perhaps go so far as to set up some informal presentations or relaxation times, even to plan "play times" that will enhance the team building. (Those interested in taking this further should refer to our book *Managing Your Team*, published by Piatkus [London].)

Are Meetings Cost-effective?

Sadly, most meetings held in companies today are probably not cost-effective. But they can be and they should be. In the companies where we have been able successfully to change the meetings culture to the one outlined in this section, we know that we have created a much more cost-effective, beneficial use of meetings.

To be effective, the meeting must achieve its purpose, whether that is to make a decision, create new ideas, or whatever. To be cost-effective, these decisions and solutions should be arrived at as quickly as possible, with as little disruption of the working day as possible and with a minimum of time wasted by participants. The balance between a discussion that is too short and one that is too long is a fine one, requiring experience and skill. Guidelines for making this decision follow.

Are There Alternatives to Meetings?

Although it is true that there is no effective alternative to a well-structured meeting called for the right purpose, there are many alternatives to some of the so-called meetings held in organizations at the present time.

Meetings are often poorly thought out and called inappropriately, resulting in wasted time, dissatisfaction, and poor decision making. As a secretary advising her boss who may be calling a meeting, you should be aware of alternatives available that are more effective for communication and learning in certain circumstances. Alternatives can be summarized as follows.

Memos

Some meetings are called simply so that one person can give information to a group of people. The group comes together, sits around the table, and the person giving the presentation simply relays the information and thanks everyone for coming, and then the meeting breaks up. That is a pathetic waste of everyone's time: the time of the delegates coming to and leaving the meeting, the disruption of their normal working day, the time it takes to set up and organize the meeting, and probably some time chasing certain people to make sure that they are going to attend. In addition to that, there may be a better use that the meeting room could be put to.

In fact if such a meeting is required at all, then it will be a briefing meeting, which involves delivery of information and some interaction, probably structured (see The briefing meeting, page 8). In the meantime, let us simply confirm that if one-way information flow is all that is required, a memo is certainly more cost-effective (though we would still recommend the structure of the briefing meeting).

E-mail memos

E-mail is an electronic form of memos (and other writings) distributed through networked computers rather than on paper. The same advantages and disadvantages of memos apply to E-mail, with perhaps one important amendment. When you, as the receiver of an E-mail message, access the message on your computer screen, a signal is transmitted back to the sender indicating that you have accessed that message. You will not therefore be able to deny receiving the message, or claim that it got lost at the back of the filing cabinet.

Advantages and disadvantages of memos and E-mail

Advantages
- More cost-effective ways of delivering information.
- Do not create unnecessary interactive discussion.
- Have a specific distribution list.
- Can be read at times convenient to individuals without disruption of working time.
- Can be reread when necessary.

Disadvantages
- May lack confidentiality as memos tend to be seen as of low priority and low importance. They tend to get left around for everyone to see, more so than minutes.
- Do not allow for interaction where some might be appropriate.

Corridor meetings

We have often been told of meetings where twelve people gather together and ten of them watch two people having a discussion. For example, when there is a problem many departments are potentially affected but it may be a problem that can actually be sorted out between, say, a departmental head and a supervisor. In fact what happens is that those two individuals sort the problem out among a few useless contributions from people who feel obliged to say something, having been called to the meeting. Ten people leave feeling very dissatisfied and two people leave with the solution that they could have devised simply by meeting in a corridor or in each other's offices.

If, as a secretary being asked to call a meeting, you find that the agenda relates only to a very small number of people compared to those being invited, confirm with your boss that you should arrange for a smaller group to meet in someone's office. The group's representative can then bring agreed proposals, if necessary, to a larger meeting and present them far more expediently.

Use of the telephone

Exactly the same rules apply to using the telephone as to using each other's offices, or corridor meetings. It may not be necessary for the two people involved to meet as they may be able to sort the problem out in a simple telephone call. Certainly where the two people concerned are in remote locations, possibly different factory sites, then even two people coming together for a meeting may not be cost-effective; a telephone call may be the best way to deal with minor difficulties.

Advantages and disadvantages of corridor/telephone meetings

Advantages

- More cost-effective than formal meetings.
- Lack formality, thereby encouraging more open discussions.
- More immediate, can be called *ad hoc*.

Disadvantages

- Lack authority: a decision may still have to be made by the full committee in a meeting before decisions taken by two people can be implemented.
- Master–slave relationship. Without a controlling, balancing chairperson, there is always the danger that one person dominates the other in a one-to-one meeting, either face-to-face or on the telephone. Psychologically, the person making the demands or invading the other person's space has certain advantages that may cause inappropriate or poorly thought-out decisions to be taken.

Telephone conferencing

In theory, a group of people can meet on the telephone if the telephone system allows for, say, ten or twelve people to all engage in conversation on one telephone link. This facility is available on many company phone systems.

However, most companies do not believe that this is an effective alternative to meetings, as there are important qualities of communication lost when communication is limited to voice only. Even the most effective chairperson is at the mercy of those who are speaking at any given time and has difficulty in making sure that she has called for opinions from those who are more naturally reticent or less forceful. We know of one situation where one person involved in such meetings, who had decided that the meetings were of limited benefit anyway, played this to his perceived advantage; he joined in the opening of the teleconference and then put the phone down and ate his breakfast, occasionally picking the phone up and making noises to indicate he was still there. Over a period of many meetings, his absence from discussions was never noticed!

In some organizations we have seen teleconferencing in use where all the people in the teleconference are in the same building. We would strongly recommend that if the involvement of twelve people is required, then a formal meeting be called.

Teleconferencing comes into its own in two ways. First, where small numbers are involved, perhaps three or four, it can work quite effectively. Second, and more importantly, where all the delegates required, whether a small number or a full meeting complement, are in different locations around the country or even around the world, then it is clearly more cost-effective for at least some of the meetings to be done by telephone rather than transporting people from country to country.

A word is needed on the advantages of fully interactive meetings. In a meeting, communication is effected between people, not only through the words they speak but also from the tone of voice they use, the eye contact between the delegates, and the body language of the delegates involved. Some communication studies have indicated that up to 80 percent of the comprehension of discussions arises through the body language and eye contact and only some 20 percent through the words spoken. As teleconferencing lacks the potential for the 80 percent, it can lead to more misunderstandings and less thorough discussions. Even with the best will in the world, and the best chairperson, it can take a good deal longer to arrive at the proper conclusion than in a fully interactive meeting.

Videoconferencing

With an increased financial outlay in advanced technology, teleconferencing is being replaced by videoconferencing, i.e., telephone conferencing with the enhancement of the ability to see the people you are speaking with.

It sounds good, but the present state of technology moves us on very little from the advantages and disadvantages of teleconferencing as set out above. The technology does not allow for eye contact, which seems to be ineffective unless people are literally face-to-face in any case. Certainly body language is restricted as people quite often formalize their body language when they know they are on camera; they become less relaxed, more rigid, and less open. This is only a slightly more comfortable form of teleconferencing.

It is interesting to note that large increases in interest in videoconferencing occur during times of civil unrest or war. During the Gulf War of the early 1990s, there was a belief that, had the conflict escalated, there would have been hijacking and terrorist attacks on aircraft. Many company directors who had previously found it very important to hold meetings of the board in places such as Rio de Janeiro (often, by some unaccountable coincidence, at the same time as the carnival!) suddenly found that they were able to deal with their meetings by videoconferencing. One telecommunications manager told us that at the end of the Gulf War there was a great deal of backtracking by directors explaining why videoconferencing had not been successful and why it would again be necessary to take the Concorde to Rio! In fact we suspect we were being told a good deal less about the merits of videoconferencing than about the hidden agendas for holding meetings in certain places at certain times; secretaries will probably be more aware than we are of this kind of motivation for holding meetings.

Advantages and disadvantages of teleconferencing/videoconferencing

Advantages
- Cheaper than transporting people around the country, or around the world.
- Quicker than transporting people around the country, or around the world.
- Can be recorded.

Disadvantages

- Difficult for the chairperson to make sure that all have their say and that people do not overly dominate conversations.
- Loss of comprehension owing to loss of body language and eye contact.

In summary

When your boss asks you to arrange a meeting, be sure that you have considered and offered her these alternatives, which may be more appropriate for learning or communication given a particular situation. Only when you have determined that bringing a group of people together around the table is the most appropriate vehicle, should you be content to call the meeting. There are many "Brownie points" available for the secretary who is able to offer constructive, alternative suggestions, and knows how to arrange them. With this one exercise alone, you can save a good deal of lost staff hours and increase people's general appreciation of the time they don't spend in meetings, or the more effective time that they do spend in meetings.

Types of Meetings

Even assuming that you do decide that bringing a group of people together into a room for a meeting is the appropriate vehicle for communication and learning, there are still four meeting styles to choose from. The decision you make is based on the objectives of the meeting. The main practical arrangements to be considered involve the seating plan.

The briefing meeting

There are many instances when a group of people need information from someone. Typically, the head of the department may want to brief his department's personnel on a particular situation, project progress, or the financial state of the company. We have already suggested that a memo or descriptive report may be all that is required. However, not allowing people a vehicle for feedback or interaction can be demoralizing or ineffective; equally, bringing a group of people together into a room where one person simply talks at them for a number of hours can be incredibly boring, no matter what the subject matter is.

We suggest that the briefing meeting is the appropriate alternative.

First, distribute the information to the committee, team, or group, along with a notice that there will be a short meeting where the presenter of the brief will take questions from the group. This allows people to absorb the information in their own time, at their own pace, and in their own way of learning. They can prepare relevant questions ahead of time, which can then be asked of the team leader to gain the specific information required. This combines the advantages of the cost-effectiveness of memos with the cost-effectiveness of a short meeting for a specific purpose.

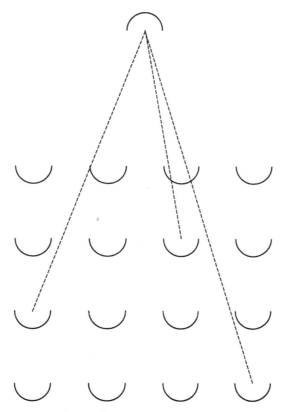

Figure 1 Seating layout for briefing meetings showing the lines of interaction between speaker and delegates.

In order to make a briefing meeting successful, we suggest the room layout shown in Figure 1. In this diagram, the chairs are laid out in theater style. All the chairs face the front and only the presenter faces the delegates. This allows for the maximum interaction between the presenter and each individual delegate, but limits the interaction between delegates and therefore limits probably irrelevant discussion.

We regularly hear that briefing meetings can be boring. You might consider an alternative to a briefing in the form of a full presentation. In this, the person will distribute some sort of brief before the presentation and then make a fully interactive presentation to the group (possibly using the theater style layout or one of the other layouts examined below), but will use the techniques of presentation to enhance the delivery. This book is not the right vehicle to describe presentation techniques but typically they would include visually exciting slides, large color photo displays around the walls, possibly music, and so on.

The addition of desks in front of the chairs turn the theater style into classroom style, allowing for the same basic dynamics. This can be more comfortable if a large number of papers or processes need to be worked through by the delegate.

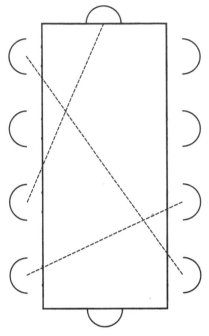

Figure 2 Seating layout for hierarchical meetings. The Long Table.

The interactive/pecking order meeting

Many corporate meetings are boardroom style, with the delegates seated around a long table as in Figure 2. Traditionally the most senior person there will take the chair and will sit at the head of the table. In hierarchical companies, others seat themselves on the basis that the more senior the person, the closer his proximity to the chairperson. The arrangement allows for fully face-to-face eye contact between all delegates and facilitates interactive discussion.

The fully interactive meeting

In more enlightened and open companies, an effective chairperson establishes his authority without the need for hierarchical devices such as the long table. Getting the most open debate from people, and the most creative suggestions, is usually facilitated with the roundtable, as demonstrated in Figure 3. Again this allows for fully interactive eye contact and the best possible atmosphere for free discussion.

Brainstorming

In order to be effective, brainstorming meetings, i.e., meetings where very creative suggestions are sought, need the minimum of formality and the maximum of interaction. The roundtable arrangement is the most effective for brainstorming. In some companies, removal of the table, with people sitting in a circle in relaxed easy chairs,

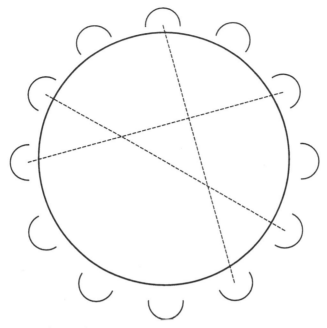

Figure 3 Seating layout for effective, open meetings. The Roundtable.

is often highly effective. The success of the brainstorming is usually dependent on the lack of barriers and the skill of the facilitator.

Training meetings

Traditionally used by trainers, the horseshoe style of layout shown in Figure 4 allows for a special kind of interaction. Here the advantages of all delegates being face to face, allowing for interaction between them, is gained. In addition, however, the trainer, or team leader, commands the direct attention of all delegates and can turn an interactive meeting quickly into a briefing style meeting. In addition, the team leader is able to move down the horseshoe and directly talk one-on-one to individual delegates. All forms of interaction are therefore catered for.

The horseshoe arrangement has another advantage. Where meetings might be potentially explosive, with high emotions between delegates, experienced facilitators know how to deflect aggression by moving down the horseshoe and breaking the eye contact between argumentative types. They position their own body between the two, and deal one-on-one with individual delegates.

In summary

When asked to set up a meeting, you should consider the type of meeting being requested and consider the room layout that best facilitates that particular communication, learning, or team building requirement. Consider the needs of all delegates and the preferences of the chairperson. We suggest that where possible, the long

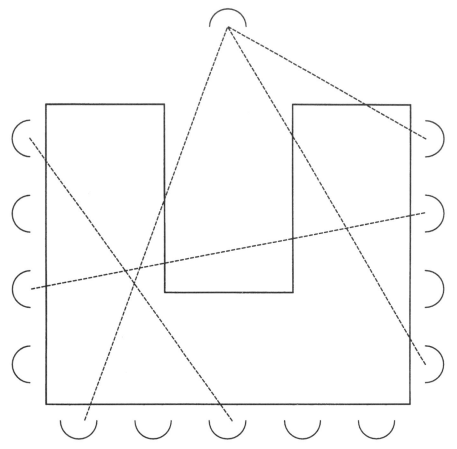

Figure 4 The Horseshoe. Used for training and some interactive discussions.

table should be replaced by the roundtable; the chairperson should be able to stamp his authority without such mechanical devices.

It may be that the meeting takes place in a room where the layout is determined by either the size of the room or simply the furniture available. In these cases, given the models to choose from, it is up to you to produce the best compromise creatively. A chairperson faced with a long table but not wishing to be seen to be playing the hierarchy game can deliberately position himself at a more random point on one of the sides, for example. You may be able to advise the chairperson about this if he is uncertain of the dynamics from which the meeting would benefit.

Types of Meetings: Minute Taking Styles

There are some broad guidelines for minute taking relating to each of the individual styles of meetings noted above.

The briefing meeting

Provided the presenter of the briefing has prepared a well-presented document, then the minutes secretary is relieved of the boredom of having to paraphrase long-winded material that is presented verbally. All the secretary needs to do is attach a copy of the circulated paper to the published minutes—the minutes themselves containing only the highlights of questions or points raised and discussed at the shortened briefing meeting.

Brainstorming

The secretary's main contribution to brainstorming meetings is not to be intrusive. Indeed, these meetings often have no formal secretaries because minute taking as such is not required. People must be free to put forward even outrageous suggestions on which others can build more practical possibilities, and they may be restricted in doing so if they know that everything said is being jotted down. In a brainstorming meeting, all that is required is a reporter's notebook kept discreetly out of sight and the jotting down of specific points to be followed up. At the end of even the most complex brainstorming meeting, the secretary should come away with no more than half a dozen or so main points that will be the subject of later follow up.

Another way to synthesize brainstorming meetings is to type up the flip chart notes, with the secretary taking no formal notes at all during the meeting, unless specifically asked to do so.

All other meetings, particularly interactive meetings

Generally, a full set of minutes should be taken and published, usually summarizing the main points of discussions, any decisions taken and any actions arising. These are the fullest published minutes and the hardest work for the minutes secretary.

Immediate need versus archive life

It will be up to the minutes secretary, taking account of the wishes of the chairperson and other delegates, to decide the appropriate level of detail of the summaries of discussions. Some discussions are of topics that have very limited duration and once a conclusion has been reached or an action decided upon and dealt with, the topic is effectively out of date. It may be that little or no summary is required of the discussions leading up to those decisions.

On the other hand, some topics are of potentially long duration and have what is known as an archive life. It may be that in five or ten years, when all the people at the meeting including the minutes secretary are no longer with the company, those minutes will be needed by someone who needs to know how a particular decision was arrived at, what considerations were discussed and so on. There may be legal reasons why this may be reviewed, possibly following a severe accident. In the case of health and safety meetings there may be requirements for minutes to be called for examination by the external body governing health and safety.

Obviously the minutes secretary is responsible for making sure that the proper level of minutes is published given the nature of the topic concerned.

Long duration minutes

Some minutes effectively form policy decisions made by committees and there needs to be some summary of these. We would suggest, as we have instigated in some companies, that minutes that form long-term policy are duplicated in a special file maintained by the minutes secretary, passed on to her successor, and regularly resummarized and distributed to an appropriate distribution list of people. Each distribution may summarize several years of these special minutes on just one or two pages, pointing out those decisions that have been taken in the past that form particularly relevant long-term company policy.

Meeting Preparations

We have already examined one of the most important arrangements for effective meetings: the design of the room layout, i.e., the positioning of chairs and tables for particular types of meetings. There are many other arrangements to be considered. The meetings secretary is the person who must make these arrangements, unless otherwise stated. In any case, we have found from experience that the secretary tends to be the person most concerned with the background to meetings, and therefore the best person to deal with the preparations. The secretary's focus is on the meeting as a whole, whereas individual delegates, including the chairperson, tend to focus on their own requirements. Take into account the following points.

Make sure that there is a proper announcement of time, date, and place of the meeting

In the case of regular meetings, the minutes of the previous meeting will usually end with an announcement of the time, date, and place of the next meeting. Remember, however, that between the publication of the previous minutes and the time of the next meeting an agenda for the next meeting will be issued and that agenda should confirm the previously made announcement. If there are changes to the time, date, and place as announced in the previous minutes, then make a special point of highlighting this and stressing the correct arrangements.

Where possible, arrange for a bigger than necessary room

It is physically possible to get a meeting of, say, ten or twelve people into a room 12 to 15 feet square. For ten to twelve people, we would suggest a room, if available, of at least 25 feet square, but bigger if possible. Cramped space leads to cramped thinking and a lack of creativity. Airy, light rooms facilitate creative, open, intelligent discussion.

Should you have a choice of many rooms or be involved in the design and layout of training and meetings suites, then also consider the advantages of large window space—giving plenty of natural light and if possible as pleasant a view as is available from the windows. One of our clients had its training suite on the top floor of a large, mid-city hotel and had arranged matters so that every training room had a panoramic view around the area. It was an extremely pleasant atmosphere to train in and we felt that it was no coincidence that the delegates on our courses were highly expressive, creative, energized people. Another of our clients had its training suite in a basement, where the only natural light came from glass panels in the ceiling looking up on to the pavement. Throughout the training day all the delegates could see were the lower legs of people passing by. It was the closest thing in modern corporate training to being a Beirut hostage! We made our criticisms known and the training suite for that company has now been moved to the fifteenth floor of a tower block. We are certain that it will have a beneficial effect on delegates.

Of course there are practical limitations imposed by budget, geography, and so on. If your meeting rooms happen to be in a block surrounded by factories then almost all views from the windows will be industrial in nature. Take the ideal advice in this section and make as much of it work as is possible or practical.

Use comfortable chairs

There is a theory in meetings that if the chairs are uncomfortable, people will be more inclined to stay awake. Actually what happens is that people are awake, but fidgeting, constantly looking at the clock for a time when they can get into a more comfortable chair. They are not paying attention to the discussion. At a lively meeting run by an effective chairperson, people will not fall asleep in even the most comfortable chairs. We suggest, therefore, that you make your meeting attendees as comfortable as possible and concentrate on the other areas detailed in this chapter to make the meeting lively, rather than resorting to what amounts to the tactics of the Spanish Inquisition.

Sometimes people can get rather carried away in trying to invent ways to shorten meetings by using a lack of comfort for the delegates. In June 1993 the *Financial Times* reported from Japan that staff at the Yokohama Town Hall were "being urged to conduct meetings standing up." A special conference room had been built without chairs and tables, which they thought would reduce the amount of time spent in meetings there.

No part of the meeting should last longer than two hours

Meetings do not work for periods longer than two to four hours at most; after that time, there is a considerable falling off of concentration or application. In the case of a four-hour meeting, make sure that there is a reasonable comfort break of 15 to 30 minutes between two sessions to allow people to reenergize themselves.

In certain cases, particularly where, for example, you have called your meeting attendees in from several countries for one meeting, it may be cost-effective and desirable to run the meeting through the whole of the day: seven to eight hours. If you do not want to waste those people's time, then make sure that you still break up the day, with no part of the meeting lasting longer than two hours without a considerable break. Make sure that you make effective arrangements for a proper break at lunchtime (see below).

Breaks must be taken away from the room

Encourage people to get up from their chairs, leave the room, and walk into another room, where tea, coffee, and other refreshments are provided. Just the act of getting up and walking about after two hours in a chair changes the level of activity of air in the lungs and blood in the circulation. After a short break, people come back to the table much fitter and more energized, with their sluggishness removed.

In the case of very long meetings, make sure that a lunch break of at least an hour's duration is arranged and make sure that people leave the room and go to another location to have their lunch. The worst possible way to run a meeting, and the way that guarantees the most sluggish, unfocused, deenergized attendees, is to have refreshment breaks and lunch breaks at the table.

At the same time, suggest to attendees that they do not use the breaks to return to their offices to see what messages have been left for them. If they do, they will de-focus themselves from the subjects of the meeting and worry about messages that have been received and about which they can probably do nothing until the following day, or after the meeting at the very least. You must take responsibility for entertaining people at the refreshment breaks in order to give the strongest possible hint that they should remain as a group while taking a break from the subject matter of the agenda.

Arrange for notepads, pens, and pencils

You must regard your meeting attendees as guests and you must seek to pander to their need for comfort and save them from embarrassment. There is no more embarrassing a position than to turn up for a meeting and have to announce that you have forgotten to bring a pen or notepad. Let it be known that you have some spare notepads and pens or pencils available and that anyone needing some spares can discreetly approach you before going into the meeting. Even better is to put some notepaper, pens, and pencils out around the table for all the attendees, who can use them or ignore them as they choose without having to draw attention to their own possible oversights.

Have spare calculators where appropriate

Unlike with notepaper, pens, and pencils, people tend to use their own calculators, but accidents can happen. For a cost of just a few dollars each, you can have some spare calculators in your drawer and again let it be known that people can borrow one from you for the meeting (make sure they return them when leaving!). It is not always a question of a person forgetting a calculator, which would be embarrassing enough at a finance meeting: sometimes people use, for example, solar-powered calculators and the lighting in the room may not be adequate for them to function. In addition to spare calculators always have spare batteries, which you can offer people who need them.

Arrange all equipment and test it before the meeting

There is probably no more embarrassing a situation than to set up an overhead projector for your boss, who stands at the front of the meeting, switches it on, and finds that the bulb and the spare bulb have both blown. You should personally set up and test all equipment before handing over the room to your chairperson, in particular the following:

- Overhead projector. Test that both bulbs are working, that the projector is pointing directly at the projection screen, and that it is focused (use a test acetate slide for this purpose). This will also ensure that you plug it in and switch it on. Make sure that you know where each of the appropriate switches is located (overhead projectors vary considerably in design) and quickly brief your chairperson if he needs some guidance.
- Flip charts. Make sure that there is adequate paper on the flip chart and that there are appropriate flip chart pens available in a variety of colors. Test each pen to see that the previous user has not let it dry up. Have a spare flip chart pad, or at least know where one is easily available.
- Whiteboards/blackboards. Make sure that these are cleaned and that you have the appropriate nonpermanent markers. Test these to make sure that they have not dried up. Make sure that you have the appropriate sponges or cloths to wipe the board clean during presentations.
- Slide projector. If anyone giving a presentation to the meeting requires 35 mm transparency slides, have a slide projector available. Test that it is working and focused as you would the overhead projector.
- VCR. During a presentation, someone may wish to play a videotape. Make sure that you have VCR and television equipment available; test that the television is switched to the video channel and that playback is correctly set. Test the volume. Make yourself familiar with the buttons on both the VCR and the television, or the remote control units, so that you can brief your chairperson or anyone giving a presentation as appropriate.

Arrange refreshments

Make sure that you have made arrangements for coffee, tea, cold refreshments, and water to be available. If you are making arrangements for lunch, make sure that the appropriate catering has been booked for that day. It is considered appropriate to provide a variety of alternatives, e.g., caffeinated and decaffeinated coffee, a selection of teas, carbonated and decarbonated mineral water, or a variety of juices. Consider special dietary requirements for lunch, such as vegetarian. Some people have special dietary needs relating to allergy or health. Although it is sensible for them to point this out to you, it is also polite if you check with your delegates to see if they have such requirements.

Etiquette suggests that vegetarianism is now so widespread that you should automatically provide vegetarian alternatives for lunch. Other specialist dietary requirements are perhaps less common and it is up to those people to notify you of their needs. However, it is still regarded as polite for you to make appropriate inquiries.

Arrange for no interruptions

Suggest to your chairperson that he or she makes announcements that the meeting is not to be interrupted except in extreme circumstances. Delegates should switch off pagers and cellular phones. In one ludicrous situation we saw, a person took a phone call on his cellular phone in a meeting and in order to be discreet went to the corner of the room to talk in private. What happened was predictable; the rest of the delegates talked louder to show that they weren't listening to his conversation, and talked absolute rubbish proving that they were! You cannot insist on all attendees emptying out their pockets of pagers and mobile phones and leaving them on your desk before they go into the room, but you can ask them to turn them off. You can ask them to leave them with you if they are expecting an important message and then you can answer the call, take a note of the message, and point out a time when the call can be returned.

Secretaries should not stick post-it notes on the glass panel in the door of the room. As soon as one of those notes is pushed on the glass, the meeting falls apart, with everyone wondering whether it's for them. You should make it clear to callers, and to attendees, that you do not expect even to give them their messages until the end of the meeting unless it is extremely urgent. You will need your chairperson's authority for this and you will have to make whatever compromises are required by him. You might point out to the chairperson that even the smallest of interruptions can break the flow of a meeting very badly and extend a discussion unnecessarily by some half an hour. Most such interruptions could have waited an hour or two.

It is, however, incumbent on you to make provision for genuinely urgent messages and make sure that you know what to do if you receive one. Know how to interrupt the meeting to deliver such a message. (See the guidance on this in Assertiveness, Part 4.)

Your Partnership with the Chairperson

This section, of necessity, restricts itself to the secretarial role in meetings but recognizes that many secretaries are able to assist and advise their bosses on meetings administration, formalities, and so on. We are not, therefore, specifically examining the qualities of the chairperson, which, we recognize, the secretary to the meeting does not require. That said, there are many areas where the chairperson-secretary partnership is evident and the secretary needs some understanding of what the chairperson is or should be doing at the meeting so as to support him effectively. (In training, we came across some evidence that perhaps we have taught this point too well—one delegate on a course based on this chapter's material later wrote to us to tell us that she had been officially appointed chairperson to all meetings in her, admittedly fairly small, company. This constituted a very positive career move for her.)

After this section, we shall be looking at the role of the secretary but it is sensible at this point to establish the secretary's position in the so-called pecking order. Many involved in a meeting would suggest that the order of priority of the people there is:

1. chairperson;
2. the other delegates;
3. (lowest of the low) the secretary.

All the evidence indicates that this is not the case. Running a meeting effectively is itself a quality job that needs to be done by specially trained people who see it as such. We believe, therefore, that the proper order is:

1. chairperson;
2. secretary;
3. the other delegates.

We should point out that the chairperson and secretary are so close as to be almost a partnership. (The other delegates may outrank the secretary in the company; this ranking order relates to meetings administration only.)

The first step toward more highly effective meetings is to recognize that the secretary of the meeting has an important role. These tasks should not be given to "the most junior person around" or (as we have seriously heard suggested in some of our client companies) "the last person to enter the room."

The following is a list of the principal qualities of an effective chairperson. The chairperson should be:

- neutral;
- knowledgeable, but not an expert;
- a coordinator;
- a firm decision maker;
- a good listener;
- a clarifier of the meeting's objectives;
- responsible to the needs of the meeting and attendees;
- a questioner;
- a harmonizer;
- a leader.

The secretary can assist the chairperson in the following ways.

Listening

Three types of listening are going on at any given time in a meeting: aware, involved, distant. A good chairperson is always *aware* listening, the participants are generally *involved* listening, and the secretary is *distant* listening. The three can be summarized as follows.

- Aware listening. The most concentrated of all listening. While the chairperson is listening to attendee A and preparing for his own response, he is also aware that attendee B may have passionate views on the subject being spoken about and will be wanting to speak. The chairperson is further aware that attendee C is naturally reticent but has important views the meeting should hear. The chairperson will be ready to draw those views together. Aware listening involves being fully aware of those who are not speaking as well as those who are. In addition, aware listening involves a responsibility to make sure that other people understand what is being said; an effective chairperson paraphrases anything being said and plays it back to the meeting, giving the person who originally spoke an opportunity to correct any misapprehensions. It also provides an opportunity for all attendees to hear the same point made in two ways, giving them a more three-dimensional understanding.
- Involved listening. When an attendee is being directly addressed by either the chairperson or another attendee, he will not only be listening to the words but also actively planning a response. Unlike in aware listening, however, he will not be so concerned about the possible responses of other attendees or the absence of responses from more reticent members.
- Distant listening. The distant listener is absorbing what is being said without planning any response or being aware of the possibility of some other contribution being made.

At different times, in the meeting, people will shift between styles. The chairperson should never, of course, be anything other than aware listening, but attendees will fluctuate between involved listening and aware listening when they are in debate about a topic for which they have strong views or commitments. During debate on those topics, they will become conscious of the possible contributions of others and they will be eager to paraphrase and play back to the meeting important points that they are concerned other people should understand fully. Attendees will also fluctuate between involved listening and distant listening in topics in which they perceive themselves as having little or no interest or involvement.

The secretary should always be distant listening, as this is the form of listening that allows for an accurate historical record to be made. However, it would be understandable for the secretary to become more involved if, for example, the subject being discussed involved some aspect of the secretarial function. Whether or not the secretary should make contributions to the meeting is a topic to be looked at shortly.

In the difference between aware listening and distant listening, we see one of the most important roles of the chairperson–secretary partnership. It is virtually impossible for the chairperson to remain aware listening if he is also concentrating on writing down notes about what is being said. By having a reliable secretary, and using distant listening to record accurately the narrative of discussion, the chairperson is free to use aware listening to keep the meeting dynamics running high, to keep the debate as a high point of interest, and to make sure that all delegates have their fair share of the discussion. If the chairperson could not rely on the secretary, then he would have to keep making sure that certain points were being noted and this would break up the flow of the meeting and dissipate its energies.

Keeping the meeting focused

The chairperson has a balance of responsibilities between keeping attendees of the meeting focused on the subject at hand and at the same time being responsive to the needs of people at the meeting. Take a situation, for example, where an attendee drives to work but on getting to work finds that she cannot park in the parking lot, or in her own appointed space, because someone has blocked it or acted rudely. She comes to the meeting—now possibly late—and feels angry that she is forced to apologize because of someone else's bad manners. She is fuming. Item 1 on the agenda relates to a project in development, of which one small incidental part is the location of the parking lot. At a particular moment, the attendee, when the rest of the meeting is concentrating on the car parking, suddenly explodes into a diatribe about bad parking, bad driving, and so on. Should the chairperson immediately stop her and point out that this is irrelevant and wasting the time of the other attendees or should he allow the person to vent her anger, possibly boring the other attendees and losing the energy of the debate? The answer is that a good chairperson will allow the attendee 30 seconds or a minute to vent her anger and then gently remind her that the meeting must get back to its original topic of discussion. The advantage is that in that period of time the other attendees will politely listen, the high energy level will not yet be lost by boredom in the group, and the troubled attendee will feel that she has vented her anger; the red haze in front of her eyes will have disappeared and she can then make more focused valuable contributions to the meeting. To have stopped her having her say at all would have left her sitting fuming throughout the whole meeting, unable to make well-presented contributions. The meeting would therefore lose some valuable input.

However, some chairpersons are not very good at this diplomatic balancing act and might let the individual go on too long. The secretary has an opportunity to assist the chairperson in the most diplomatic ways. She should not ask the meeting or the chairperson if this point being spoken about is relevant or not; that would be rude and usurp the authority of the chairperson. However, the secretary has a duty to record accurately the views of the meeting and can politely ask (although already knowing the answer!), "Should I be jotting this down?" The chairperson, or even another attendee, will hastily point out that the secretary should not, and this will give the meeting the opportunity to draw itself back to its focus. The secretary is in a unique position to perform this diplomatic act as she has the duty and responsibility of accurate recording and can therefore get away with asking this question when perhaps other members of the group would be offensive if they did so. A golden rule of secretarial diplomacy is encompassed here: never embarrass your chairperson. Never criticize the chairperson; just ask questions pertinent to your task and leave the chairperson to use your question as his own way of regaining control of the debate.

Keeping harmony

There will sometimes be occasions in meetings when tempers run high and the debate becomes hotheaded and emotional. There is usually a peacemaker somewhere in the group and if there is not the chairperson should adopt the role, given his natural or positional authority. However, there are times when it seems that a meeting gets out of control and the chairperson either does not or cannot intervene constructively. As secretary you have an opportunity to assist your chairperson in this situation. It is your task to note down the facts in any debate for the minutes. In hotheaded, high-tempered debates, the facts are usually subordinate to conviction, opinion, belief, and so on. No one ever got emotional over facts, only the subjective interpretation of the facts. From your intervention in the debate with a seemingly innocent question—"I just want to be sure I am getting the correct facts down. Could you please list the main facts again for me?"—one of three things will happen:

1. The combatants will have to respond to your request and go over the facts. This will immediately cool tempers.
2. The chairperson will use the opportunity of your question to remind the meeting that tempers are running a bit high and it would be better to take a short break, which can then be created through taking the time to give you the facts requested (which of course you may well already have written down in your notepad!).
3. Peer pressure from around the group will allow people to react to your question by reminding others that tempers are running high and that it is the facts that are important.

One way or another, your question will almost certainly allow the group to refocus itself constructively. A further possibility is that the chairperson will use the opportunity to get some more facts relevant to the topic from other noncombatants in the group, further cooling the tempers. The golden rule is that people do not get emotional over facts, and you can legitimately demand facts as part of your task without being subject to criticism.

The Role of the Secretary

Having looked at meetings and some general rules to make them more effective, we can now look at the specific role of the secretary within that meeting. The secretary has to carry out the following tasks.

Deal with the details

We have already suggested that it is the secretary who is responsible for the preparations of the meeting, unless otherwise stated. Sometimes the chairperson prefers to deal with this or may want her own office secretary rather than the meetings secretary (if not the same person) to deal with it. However, if you accept the role of secretary, then you should accept that this is your role by default unless you are certain otherwise.

Prepare and distribute the notice of the meeting and the agenda

Agenda preparation is a separate topic looked at later in this chapter. It is the secretary's responsibility to distribute the notice of the meeting and an appropriately produced agenda. In producing the agenda, the secretary will work closely with the chairperson. The secretary is the person to whom other attendees will report matters relating to the meeting; for example, they will give notice of their own absence if applicable, report the progress of action points, and so on. Because the secretary has notice of who is available, and when, she is best able to assist the chairperson in ordering the topics on the agenda (see Agendas: How to Do It, page 45). Primarily it is the chairperson who is responsible for selecting the topics to be discussed (including suggestions made by other members of the meeting passed through the secretary). The secretary can also remind the chairperson of items brought forward from previous meetings, her own agreed priorities, and so on.

Take and distribute the minutes

Minute taking and minute publishing are covered in two separate sections in this part of the book. We will take this opportunity to stress that these tasks are the responsibility of the secretary. All too often secretaries see themselves as only some sort of service function to the rest of the meeting, almost a slave of the meeting to be ordered about at its behest. Sometimes they see themselves as a sort of personal slave of the chairperson, subject to the chairperson's orders and whims. We must point out that secretaries should insist that the role they have has its own quality with its own responsibilities. Just as the purchasing director would not generally expect to be criticized or overridden by the sales director, and the sales director would not generally expect to be criticized or overridden by the finance director, so the secretary, having taken the minutes properly and published them truly and correctly, should not be subject to criticism by members of the meeting, who all too often manipulate the minutes to read the way they want them to. Napoleon described history as a "collection of lies agreed upon"; the minutes of the meeting—after the meeting is over—are all that remain of the meeting and they become its true history whether or not they are accurate. The secretary should insist that if he or she does a quality job that job should be respected. Secretaries can of course make mistakes, but there is an opportunity to correct them as the minutes of the previous meeting are always examined at the beginning of the next meeting, giving an opportunity for challenge in the meeting forum. An inappropriate challenge might aim to manipulate the secretary's opinion of a debate outside the meeting structure.

These comments also apply to the chairperson, although the secretary may have a diplomatic balancing act to perform to insist on the chair respecting the secretarial function (see What Do You Do if the Chairperson Asks You to Falsify Minutes?, see page 26).

Assist and advise the chairperson on rules of debate

In most meeting formats there are few rigid rules of debate other than politeness, respect for the authority of the chair, and so on. However, there are certain meetings where there are strict rules (for example, trade union meetings tend to run to a more rigid format). If you are accompanying your boss to one of these meetings, or perhaps to a meeting in another company, there may be some Brownie points to be had by telephoning your opposite number at that location and finding out if there are any special rules that ought to be considered.

Remind the meeting of obligations and confidentiality

It is first and foremost the chairperson's responsibility to make sure that people at the meeting are aware of the level of confidentiality of given subjects. However, if the chairperson fails to do this, the secretary can either remind her of that requirement or at the end of the meeting make the point as part of the secretary's role.

Of course, all matters discussed in company meetings are private and should not be discussed elsewhere, at least without specific permission, but occasionally topics have a special level of confidentiality that needs to be reinforced. For example, one of our client companies' sites emitted a large visible gas cloud, which, though harmless, caused some concern in the local community. There were several meetings about this, but the chairperson was concerned that there should be no discussion of this topic as a proper announcement was to be made through a press conference later that week. Therefore, this special level of confidentiality had to be reinforced to the attendees and could have been done, if not by the chairperson, then by the secretary.

We were told of a story that came from the days when banks were legally allowed not to disclose their profits even to their own shareholders. At the annual general meeting, a shareholder asked what the profits were and the chairperson pointed out he could not answer that. A second person, probably primed, then asked what corporation tax had been paid and the chairperson, not having been told that this was confidential, began to prepare the answer. It was an alert secretary who reminded the chairperson that corporation tax is directly related to profits and by disclosing one he would indirectly be disclosing the other. This was of course a specialist situation and it was the company secretary doing the secretarial role at that time. However, the meetings secretary who arms herself with some specialist knowledge that can be of use to the chairperson gains the respect of all at the meeting.

Deal with action points arising

Consider a situation where at a previous meeting John has agreed to take on a certain task and report back to the next meeting. When the chairperson is going through the appropriate topic on the next meeting's agenda and asks John for his report, John announces that he has not done the task. Who is at fault in this situation? It is tempting to consider that John is at fault, but a moment's reflection will show that this is not the case. John may well be at fault for not doing the task and will presumably be properly reprimanded for it. However, the task under discussion is the proper construction of an agenda and we have already pointed out that this is a quality product of the secretarial function. It could be that certain people have been invited to the meeting just to hear John give his proposals and they have now wasted their time and possibly, in the ripple effect, have extended some other debates by feeling the compulsion to contribute when their views were probably not that valid. If there was no reason for inviting them—and John not having done his task means that they were not necessary—then the secretary should not have invited them. It is the secretary who has failed to produce a proper, effective, agenda for the meeting. The buck stops somewhere and in the case of the agenda it stops with the secretary.

In summary, the above tasks are the responsibility of the secretary, either directly or as a backup to the chairperson's own responsibilities.

Can the Secretary Contribute to Debates in Meetings?

Whether or not secretaries are encouraged to contribute to meeting debates is usually a function of company culture; however, we suggest a few observations for secretaries to consider, and for them to put to the chairperson or meetings generally.

First, we would stress, as we have already said, that the secretary is an important part of the meeting, indeed second only and close to the chairperson if the meeting is to have high energy dynamics. The secretary's main function is to take away from the chairperson certain duties, allowing the chairperson to perform at the highest level of involvement. Because of this, particularly as the secretary is distant listening, there is less opportunity for the secretary to contribute than any other attendee. This has to be recognized from the outset.

In one client company, the meetings secretary was not allowed to sit at the table with the other delegates but had to sit at her own table in the corner. This was a totally improper attitude and a failure of recognition of the role. For one thing, for good comprehension of the meeting, the secretary has to be able to study the body language of the attendees and has to have the maximum chance to hear clearly what they are saying (see Listen in blocks and then paraphrase, page 30). Second, there are many roles where the secretary and chairperson complement each other; we would always recommend that the secretary is positioned next to the chairperson.

We also have to recognize that the secretary is probably less involved in the day-to-day dealings of particular agenda topics and therefore will have less likelihood of valuable contributions to make.

All that said, however, there will be times when the secretary has a valuable contribution to offer, because the subject being discussed is relevant to the secretarial function or relevant to the person's own experience, or because—however much the rest of the meeting might like to disregard it—secretaries have the most efficient communication networks in any company. The meeting that uses those communication networks is more efficient than one that ignores them. In one client company, a secretary listened to a debate about freezer foods and the packaging that attracted shoppers to their particular products. Convinced that not one of the people around the table had ever wheeled a shopping cart, she offered her own observations from 30 years of shopping. She was castigated for making a contribution, but, we discovered, the meeting authorized a firm of consultants to spend an extremely large sum of money to confirm what she had already told them! We are not suggesting that life experience is the only, or even the most important, contribution to a debate, and the opinions of experienced and trained experts are of course invaluable. However, the meeting chose to disregard a small contribution that would have been of value to it almost certainly because it came from the secretary rather than from one of the other attendees. That perception of secretaries is a waste of resource.

We would therefore suggest that secretaries have less opportunity to make contributions, will probably seek to make fewer contributions than most, cannot make long or complicated presentations as they would detract them from their main function at the meeting, but should be respected when they choose to make the few contributions that are available to them.

What Do You Do if the Chairperson Asks You to Falsify Minutes?

Being asked to falsify minutes is one of the most severe dilemmas that a secretary can encounter. We suggest that secretaries must determine their own level of integrity and decide whether they are prepared to be used as a tool to manipulate others or whether secretaries stand, as we recommend, on the responsibility and quality of the job as an end in its own right.

Of course there will always be compromises. The chairperson or a member of the meeting looking at recorded minutes might suggest that the secretary has overemphasized or underemphasized a certain point. This is clearly a matter of opinion and the secretary will have to use diplomatic skills to decide whether or not the minutes would be better published in one way or another. Company politics, while they are a problem, cannot be ignored; they are a fact of life. However, there is a considerable difference between that and a situation where a secretary is asked to leave out a complete area of debate or topic, or even to change the end result from one thing to another.

Consider where the responsibility lies. If the minutes are challenged as incorrect, it will be the secretary who takes responsibility and will be thought of as incompetent. The person who has asked the secretary to lie is unlikely to own up, even if, or perhaps particularly if, it is the chairperson. And remember there will be challenges: the minutes of the meeting are subject to scrutiny and confirmation at the next meeting.

We suggest that secretaries make clear their integrity from the outset and establish with the chairperson that they will not lie. We further suggest establishing a relationship that recognizes the secretarial function as a quality job in its own right and not as a support service to the meeting.

Other practical steps that the secretary can take are to agree that recorded minutes will not be circulated before proper circulation, and that the secretary will accept the responsibility for criticism if and when it is appropriate. However, it may be agreeable to circulate recorded minutes relating to specific topics to certain people to make sure that they are as accurate as possible. It should be agreed at that time that any amendments suggested by individuals will be noted as such, so that, should they be challenged, the person responsible can be indicated in the meeting. This will reduce the probability of anyone deliberately trying to manipulate the minutes.

Note Taking During Meetings

The main purpose of minute writing is to provide a factual record of the meeting. The style of writing should reflect this and therefore the note taking you make during the meeting must lead to this. It has been said of meetings that an efficient secretary can leave the meeting with the minutes virtually ready for publication without editing. This is naive and reflects a lack of understanding about the value of editing before publication. As pointed out in Powerful and Persuasive Writing (Part 3), 80 percent of the effort in a good document goes into the editing rather than the recording. The time you as secretary spend making the publishable minutes readable, comprehensible, and informative saves all the minute readers valuable time and prevents dissatisfaction.

We suggest that the following points relating to your work in the meeting will assist you in producing highly effective minutes.

Distinguish between fact and opinion

We are not suggesting that one is more correct for publication than the other, as facts or opinions may be relevant, but it is important when publishing the minutes to make clear whether you are publishing an authoritative fact that, by definition, cannot be challenged or whether you are publishing a person's opinion, which is therefore subject to debate. You will not always have very clear clues as to whether a person is expressing facts or their opinion; the only clue we can really offer is that when someone thumps the table and shouts, "That's a fact!", he or she is almost certainly expressing an opinion.

Sometimes you will have to challenge in your own mind what you are hearing. Take these two phrases:

"This is a good word processor"

"I think this is a good word processor."

It appears at first glance that the first is a fact and the second is an opinion but a moment's reflection will reveal that the opposite is true. "Good" is not an objective statement but a subjective one and not itself factual. The statement "This is a good word processor" must therefore be the opinion of the person speaking and you should not be fooled into reporting support for that particular word processor; rather you should indicate that it was one person's opinion that it was a good word processor. This would be different from the statement "This is an IBM word processor." That is clearly a fact as it is not a subjective point. On the other hand, the second statement—"I think this is a good word processor"—although it expresses an opinion, and is therefore clearer for you to identify, is also factual because it reflects quite openly the fact of the person's opinion. The subtlety is as follows. The first phrase may be used by someone to sway others toward the same opinion and may be delivered in such a way as to make a challenge difficult, so that the person gets his own way. The second statement is open and honest and does not create a barrier to another person saying that she does not hold the same opinion.

In summary, facts are objective rather than subjective and your presentation of them is not difficult. Opinions are subjective and you must present them in such a way as to show their subjectivity, as well as leaving open the door for appropriate counterarguments without unwittingly being someone else's tool of persuasion.

Be selective

You will not be able to write everything down, nor should you try to do so. You must be selective and jot down what is relevant. You are looking at the balance between "nice to know" end "need to know." You should eliminate the nice to know and report only the need to know, i.e., the important points of discussion raised. Experience is vital in making these decisions and that comes with practice. However, there is one very useful tool relating to key words that helps considerably in determining the need to know from the nice to know. Many agenda items involve debating choices between alternatives. Find the key phrases that determine those alternatives and divide your notepad into an appropriate number of columns (it will usually be no more than two or three). As you are listening to the debates, note each one in its appropriate column. Any point raised that does not fit into only one of the columns but could equally fit into all of the columns is not relevant in arriving at any decision.

Consider as an example for this selection process the item: "Whether to lease or buy the replacement computer equipment recommended in the IT budget for the forthcoming budget year."

First you must find the key words in this heading. The key words represent the choice, and the choice in this section is whether to lease or buy. You should therefore divide your notepad into two columns, one headed "lease" and the other "buy." When an attendee raises the point that leasing will cost $80,000 annually, that can clearly be put into the "lease" column as it relates to that and not to buying. Similarly, the tax advantages on capital allowances that will follow from outright purchase would be noted in the "buy" column as they do not relate to leasing. However, when a delegate suggests that "The APW Computer Company, Ltd. provides computers with built-in antireflectance screens," it is clear that these computers could be leased or purchased and therefore this fact, however interesting, is not relevant to the discussion of whether to lease or buy. Therefore, it need not be noted.

Sort out ambiguities during the meeting

There are two very practical reasons why you should challenge any ambiguities in your mind while you are note taking.

First, if you make a mental note to check with Simon after the meeting what it was he meant so that you can jot down his views accurately, you can bet that nine times out of ten Simon will not be available to talk to you after the meeting, or he will be called away early. Secretaries who have tried this technique become convinced that key people are always spirited away at the appropriate time by the same gremlins that always arrange for the telephone to ring when you are in the shower!

Second, and more importantly, we can start from the knowledge that you are an intelligent person. The odds are that if you do not understand fully, without ambiguity, a point being made then a few other people in that room will not do so either. They may be embarrassed and not wish to show their ignorance by asking for the ambiguity to be cleared up. However, you have the responsibility for accuracy and can use that as your legitimate reason for questioning. When you do ask the question, take a look around the room; the odds are that you will visualize lightbulbs lighting up over the heads of several people.

Keep pace with the meeting

During a debate on point 6 of the agenda, do not suddenly ask a question relating to point 4. Such an inquiry will destroy the flow of the current debate and lose the focus of the meeting. Be sure that you have answered all your own queries relating to each topic before the chairperson moves on. If necessary, agree with your chairperson that before moving on to the next item he will always quickly check with you that you are content with your notes.

Use the agenda as your format
for note taking and minute publishing

For a variety of reasons, the chairperson may decide to take point 6 after point 4 and come back to point 5 later. Do not be tempted to leave a couple of blank pages in your notepad to deal with point 5. In those circumstances, those same gremlins will make sure that that debate overruns. If your heading for each topic is clear, then you will be able to reshuffle your notes into the agenda order before publishing.

We recommend that you publish the minutes in the order of the agenda and not in the order of discussion if there is a difference. The agenda for the meeting can then be matched to the minutes at a later date. (We heard of one ludicrous situation where the debate was taken so much out of order and the minutes secretary got so confused that in order to bring the agenda and the minutes as published into line, a new agenda was published to match the minutes. Nothing could be more ridiculous than to have two different agendas for the same meeting.)

Jot down the names of the main contributors
for your notes even if they are not to be published

Even if you are not proposing to publish the name of a particular attendee alongside his opinion, it may still be useful for you to jot down people's names next to their contribution so that you can better remember who said what when you are rewriting the minutes.

Listen in blocks and then paraphrase

When people are speaking, they tend to ramble, get sidetracked, or vacillate. Nervous speakers will tend to respond to the eye contact and body language of the rest of the group and, in short, will often make a poor presentation of the main points they want to express. A verbatim record of such a delivery would be unprofessional on your part and of very limited use to readers of minutes, and would probably shock the person who had been speaking when she read it in cold black-and-white. As the minutes secretary, your job is to synthesize the main points for the readers. This can be done in one of two ways, only one of which is recommended. The wrong approach, often a mistake of secretaries with shorthand capability, is to write down virtually everything being said and then to do the synthesis at the word processor later. This creates all sorts of problems in that it does not allow you to sort out ambiguities during the meeting (see above). In fact, many secretaries who can take shorthand do not do so in taking minutes simply because this removes the temptation to write at the same speed that the speaker speaks. If you can take shorthand, and can be disciplined, you should not let your ability to "write at speed" cloud your judgment over synthesis then and there in the meeting. The correct way to take notes and synthesize is to listen in blocks and paraphrase the main points as you go.

Blocks can be identified by body language and vocal shifts. During any passage of any length people will build up to a point, usually with noncritical irrelevancies, and having made the point will taper away similarly. The vocal shift in their voice will tell you of the importance they attach to what they are saying and you can identify areas they regard as most important. For example, a person leaning forward raising his voice and thumping the table is clearly making a deliberately different impact from someone who is leaning back in his chair and talking slowly while gazing at the ceiling with a soft reminiscent smile on his face. During the build up and wind down phrases, you can summarize your main points so as to be ready to begin listening to the next point from that or another contributor. In heated arguments, these build up and wind down phrases are reduced if not eliminated, and it is at these times that you may have to ask the chairperson to give you a moment to clarify certain points.

Acquire an appropriate level of expertise

It is not necessary for either the chairperson or the secretary to be an expert in the subjects being discussed. Experts have a great deal of knowledge in a very small range of areas and are usually called into meetings to give their expert opinion, on which broader decisions can be taken by those with a broader perspective. However, secretaries to a meeting, and particularly one including technical or specialist discussions, will need to acquire a certain level of background knowledge so that they can keep pace with the discussion without having to ask for clarifications of meaning.

What you should not do is read library books! The secretary should not try to learn the level of expertise needed by reading technical books, journals, and so on, as these will probably confuse more than they will clarify. An even worse problem may be summed up by the expression "a little knowledge is a dangerous thing"; you may end up misunderstanding or using phrases incorrectly because the meaning is not clear to you in context.

What you should do is read the previous minutes of the same meetings, which will have, in context, the sorts of level of discussion that you will be subject to. In addition, it may be useful to discuss the subject with one or two of the people from the meeting in less formal surroundings. You can be quite clear about your reasons; ask them to go over some of the background to a particular point in an environment, perhaps your own office, where you can question more thoroughly points that you do not understand.

In the end expertise comes, as it always does, with experience, and the more meetings you attend the more appropriate a level of expertise you will naturally acquire.

Some meetings are of a technical nature, i.e., meetings of engineering groups, chemical groups, and so on, and there will be a lot of jargon and specialist terms being used. In addition to the above suggestions, you could also consider creating your own glossary of the main jargon, which you take to meetings. You will find that over time, you simply refer to the glossary less and less as you have picked up the understanding in context. However, the glossary will be a useful starting point and, for a while, a confidence booster. Indeed, the act of creating a glossary clarifies many points even before you attend your first meeting.

Minute Publishing Style

The main purpose of minute writing is to provide a factual record of the meeting; the style of publishing should reflect this.

Simple words and short sentences

People read minutes to overview quickly what happened at a meeting, to make sure that they are aware of decisions taken and actions to be taken, and to keep up-to-date with company progress. Being busy—and all managers either are busy or like to project the image of being so—they prefer to read one word instead of five. Simple words and short sentences are clear and to the point and fulfill all the basic needs of the minute reader.

There is another more subtle reason why you should always use simple words and short sentences. You cannot express anything in simple words and short sentences that you do not fully understand; we use complex words and long rambling sentences when we are on unsure ground and are, albeit subconsciously, building in ambiguity to what we are saying or writing in order not to be found out. If you can synthesize someone's main points into simple words and short sentences, it will confirm to you that you have understood not only what has been said but what you want to express to the group through the minutes.

Use expressions that are direct and to the point

Going along with simple words and short sentences are simple descriptions. There are no Pulitzer prizes for minutes and the only applause you will get will be for easy to read, well-synthesized documents. Do not be tempted to write "The meeting closed as the sun went down over the cooling towers"; if it finished at 7 P.M., say so.

As well as using expressions that are direct and to the point, avoid ambiguity by choosing words that are capable of only one interpretation. Just as above, we choose words capable of separate interpretations only to mask our own lack of focus or knowledge.

Use objective language, avoiding value judgments

When you find yourself noting phrases such as "*They seemed* to be of the opinion that . . .*" and "*They appeared* to think that . . . ,*" you are falling into the trap of exposing your own inadequacies. First, subjective opinions such as "they seemed" or "they appeared" are of little value to the minute reader as the reader does not particularly want your opinion of what was going on at the meeting but rather wants a clearer consensus from the meeting itself. If you find yourself noting "they seemed," "they appeared," and so on then stop and clarify the position with the meeting. You may find that your opinion of what they seemed to want is completely different from the one that, when challenged, they will express. You might talk to the chairperson to make sure that you are jotting down what reflects the attitude of the meeting, or you might ask the group itself to clarify some point or other. If there is genuine disagreement, then jot down roughly the numbers of people in favor of each side of the argument, or give some idea of the strength of views by checking your own opinions with the meeting as a whole. If you are to record accurately what happened at the meeting, then you have the right to ask them to assist you in clarifying certain points.

Avoid "shared world" knowledge

The "shared world" is discussed more fully in Part 3. It refers to the situation where all the people in the meeting have similar knowledge but the meeting minutes may be designed for people without that knowledge. Although the people in the meeting have a shared world image of the points being discussed, readers of the minutes beyond that group might not have. As secretary, you should make sure that your minutes are readable to your readers. You may have to find out if you have readers who will not be familiar with certain jargon, certain specialist terms, certain concepts, and so on, and you may need to spell them out in greater detail than would be needed just for the group itself.

Use reported speech, not direct quotes

There are two good reasons for using reported speech. First, if you directly quote people you will have endless arguments, with them saying something like "Yes, I agree you have not misrepresented me but I didn't actually say this, I said that . . ." People will accept a representative paraphrase of what they have said but will often challenge verbatim quotes, usually to no good point.

Second, the psychology of the meeting is that although there are individuals with individual opinions within the room, the meeting should be viewed as a united group from outside the meeting room. The meeting should therefore present itself as an entity in itself rather than as a group of individuals. Depersonalizing speech into paraphrases, i.e., reported speech rather than direct quotes, strengthens the image of the meeting as the unit in its own right. Also consider that people are self-conscious and will tend not to express their true feelings if they believe they are going to be reported verbatim, whereas they will be quite happy for their opinions to be reported with some group anonymity.

Name participants only in very special circumstances

Because the group should present a united image to the outside world and because people are likely to feel more free to express themselves with group anonymity, your minutes should not name the participants every time they express a particular point or opinion. Indeed, the minutes should give anonymity to contributors to discussions throughout. There are, however, certain circumstances when naming participants is unavoidable.

- In lists of people attending the meeting or who have given apologies for absence.
- Action points. Clearly the minutes have to identify the individuals who have volunteered to take certain actions.
- Identifying expertise. Sometimes a person is called to a meeting as a technical expert to express expert opinion or to give expert input to a discussion. Anyone reading the minutes and needing to take action on an item that has been discussed may need to go back to the technical expert on the subject and for this reason that person should be identified. However, there are still occasions when the experts are identified in the minutes as having made a particular point (i.e., points of expertise) and times when their anonymity should be treated in the same way as that of any other participant (i.e., when they are expressing a more general opinion, in the same way as other participants).
- When the person speaking demands it. This should never be a response to someone's ego to "see his name in lights" but there will be occasions when a person has a right to make his point without group anonymity. For example, a group may be deciding whether or not to build a large plant where, say, high gas pressures will be a factor in its working. One of the group may feel that this is dangerous to, say, the nearby town in the locality, and may say that although he is prepared to go along with a democratically given decision (i.e., if the group decides to go ahead with the plant), he wants it noted in the minutes that he expressed reservations as to its danger. With such a demand, it is the duty of the secretary to reflect that point in the person's name.

Exercise 1

Find a willing friend or relative who can assist you in this process. That person should read passages from a factual book (a book on astronomy, geography) and you should take notes synthesizing important points from the reading and then check back to see that you have missed no important areas.

Exercise 2

Do the same as the above using a fictional book, which obviously contains a lot more irrelevancies from the point of view of the kind of information needed at meetings. Your job will be to synthesize out everything other than the equivalent of what would be expected at a business meeting. Many fictional books have very few pertinent facts but by the same token their long-winded emotional rambling style often matches what you will hear around the meetings table!

Minute Types

There are four types of minutes that can be published, one of which is irrelevant in business and the other three of which should be clearly distinguished in our published minutes if we are to achieve our goal of high-quality, 30-second minutes. The four types are detailed below.

Verbatim minutes

This is a word-for-word recording of everything said in a meeting. It is irrelevant in business in most circumstances. Minutes should be synthesized, for the reasons given above. Verbatim minutes are used routinely in two situations: the proceedings of legislative bodies (Congress, the Houses of Parliament, etc.) are recorded verbatim, and the person playing the "piano" at the front of the court—actually a stenographer—is recording verbatim the proceedings of the court. There are limited circumstances in which verbatim records can be used in minutes, such as an accident inquiry taking statements from witnesses, or statements taken at disciplinary hearings. In these cases, it may be appropriate to make recordings or to make sure that you, or a person designated to do the work, have shorthand skills. In these rare circumstances where verbatim records are kept, there is no reason why you should not ask the person speaking to stop and allow you to keep pace with him or her; it is usually in both parties' interests. However, for the type of meeting that we are generally discussing in this chapter, verbatim recording is to be avoided.

Narrative minutes

Narrative minutes give a fuller picture of the debate, including an account of discussions leading up to decisions and the views expressed by various members of the meeting or committee. They can be difficult to write for all the reasons given in the above paragraphs, but they are the archived record of discussions that exists after the meeting has finished. It is important in many cases to have well-written narrative minutes because in several years' time people may not just want to know what decisions were made at the meeting but how professionally they were made, i.e., whether all the points were discussed, whether proper experts were brought in, and so on.

Resolution/decision minutes

Resolution/decision minutes should record only the decisions taken at the meeting and not the discussions leading up to those decisions, which should have been set out in the narrative minutes, as noted above.

Action minutes

Action minutes are to ensure that members of the meeting are reminded of actions that they have volunteered to take or that have been delegated to them (often in their absence!). (One company told us that the main reason people attend meetings is to avoid having actions made in their name.)

Summary

The strength of well-published minutes is that the three valid types of minutes—narrative minutes, decision minutes, and action minutes—are clearly separated. Following this section, we present the same set of minutes, published first how they should not be, and second how they should. Take a look at the difference between the two and you will see the visual impact of well-presented minutes. We will examine the content of the minutes shortly; for the moment consider the presentation only.

In the section Minute Publishing: How It *Should* Be Done, you will see that there are several paragraphs, each of which starts with key words or phrases that set out what the paragraph contains. Each paragraph is separated by a one-line space. The decision minutes are clearly identified by a two-line space on either side of each minute and by being started by the phrase *IT WAS DECIDED*. The action points are similarly separately identified with a two-line space on either side and the word "action" in capital letters and italicized: *ACTION*. The action minutes are further emphasized by a blank right-hand column, known as the action column, into which the name (or initials) of the person who has volunteered or been volunteered for the action is inserted.

This type of presentation plays to the psychology of reading. First, the eye needs white space in order to rest between absorbing concepts. When there are one- and two-line white space breaks, the eye can read in blocks, absorb and understand, rest, and then move on to the next block. If you compare "How it should be done" to "How it should not be done," you can see that it is very difficult to read the huge unorganized paragraph simply because it is too much to absorb in one easy read. In Part 3, we present a full page of typing with no breaks whatsoever; the effect is rather like walking down a moving escalator. Without white space, the eyes find it difficult to create the patterns needed to comprehend what is being read.

Use of the italicized capitalized phrases *IT WAS DECIDED* and *ACTION* creates patterns that the eye can immediately seek out; these are further emphasized by the double white space breaks around them. This is based on what we have termed the "yellow Lego brick effect" following experiments we conducted. The experiment is a very simple one to explain. We would put a pile of over a thousand children's gray building bricks, each with four connecting studs, in a heap on a table. We would then tell the experimenter group that one of the bricks had just two connecting studs and they had to find it. This of course took quite a long time. However, when we made the two-stud brick a yellow one and told them they were looking for a yellow brick they found it almost instantly. The mind created a pattern of a yellow brick, sought it out, instantly compared one to the other and was able to find the necessary item (we were able to test this further by inserting into the block a four-stud yellow brick and telling them they were looking for a two-stud yellow brick; many people actually grabbed the brick and held it aloft proudly before they realized that it was not what they had been asked to find). To get back to the minutes, the use of the italicized capitalized phrases *IT WAS DECIDED* and *ACTION* creates a pattern in the minutes and over time people will simply identify that pattern with decision minutes and action minutes and will be able to seek it out very quickly

The overall effect is that no matter how long the minutes, and they could run 20 to 30 pages or more, they can still be scanned effectively in 30 seconds. Any reader can flip through the pages, checking in the following order:

1. Any occurrence of his or her own name or initials in the action column.
2. Every other name or set of initials in the action column (both of these can quickly be checked across to see what action is to be taken, given the word *ACTION* on the left).
3. All the decisions taken at the meeting.

For most readers of minutes, this quick synthesis, i.e., what decisions have been taken and what actions are being taken, is all that is needed to get an appropriate overview of the meeting. It also means that relocating those points at some later time is quick and easy. This is what we mean by 30-second minutes.

There are going to be people who will need to read the detailed narratives but these are frankly few and far between. The reason for these narratives is usually one of archive value or examination during postmortem, possibly many years later. Even those who do need to read some narrative minutes will probably not have to read the narrative minutes of every point. For example, they may need to have a greater level of knowledge of, say, point 6 and they may have to read the narratives of point 6 but they will not have to read the narratives of points 1 to 5. On the other hand, someone else may need to read the narratives of point 4 but may not need 1 to 3 or 5 and 6. Out of a group of 20, there will be very few people who will need to read more than one or two narrative minutes, and in many meetings none at all.

The reason business people often demand very reduced, very abbreviated minutes is because they do not like to have to wade through tons of narrative to find the decisions and actions and they are therefore prepared to sacrifice the narrative. Our style of user-friendly minutes is one of the few areas in business where we can "have our cake and eat it too." You can have as detailed a set of narratives as you want without interfering with the quick and easy review of the minutes, which is all that is mostly required. The immediate use of the minutes is therefore secured, as is the library, or long-term, value.

Of course, none of this should be taken as an excuse for allowing long rambling narratives to be published; the same rules of short sentences, clear unambiguous words, and well-synthesized note taking still apply.

Minute Publishing: How It *Should Not* Be Done

Minutes of a meeting

Point 6

Whether to lease or buy the replacement computer equipment recommended in the IT budget for the forthcoming year.

It was felt that the $80,000 outlay could be absorbed within the current cash flow and no extra financing would be needed. A loan from the bank would be at 4 percent above the bank base rate for any purchasing. Approximately 60 terminals will need to be obtained in the next year to meet the company's IT needs. If purchased outright, we could get a discount of 14 percent from our usual supplier, APW Computer Supplies, Ltd. This would cause some cash flow difficulties; it might be necessary to obtain extra bank borrowings for these purchases. If the terminals were leased, there would be an initial outlay of approximately $80,000 in the first quarter of the budget year. Maintenance contracts have proved expensive and the company would need to consider that it would be paying for repairs and servicing after the first two years of the equipment's life. Under leasing arrangements, our suppliers have offered a service contract throughout the four-year life of the lease. The disadvantage of the lease is that there is a higher cost, though this may be offset by maintenance bills in later years if the units were purchased. Another disadvantage is that the "upgrade" figures at the end of the leases would be such that it would be difficult to leave the leasing company without expensive end-of-lease payments. This would effectively mean that the company was "tied in" to that supplier for a long-term period. Mark Digby circulated a detailed summary of his investigation into the respective purchases or leases of the terminals; a copy of his presentation document is appended to these minutes. The finance director, Bob Jones, will negotiate an additional loan from Snatchit Bank based on Mr. Digby's expenditures. Mr. Gabble asked if we had considered Zip computers; he used to have a games model they produced years ago, and he and his children had had great fun with it. Their new range included Windows-based software already bundled into the package. It was decided that the company would purchase the units needed during the next budget year. The company would arrange with its bankers to provide the additional funds necessary for these purchases. Mark Digby will summarize the exact units needed and the final expenditures. This will be presented to the next meeting. APW Computer Supplies, Ltd. have supplied figures relating to the finance company they use but these were considered too expensive compared to available bank finance.

Minute Publishing:
How It *Should* Be Done

Minutes of a meeting   *ACTION*

Point 6

Whether to lease or buy the replacement computer equipment recommended in the IT budget for the forthcoming year.

Approximately 60 terminals will need to be obtained in the next year to meet the company's IT needs.

Mark Digby circulated a detailed summary of his investigation into the respective purchases or leases of the terminals; a copy of his presentation document is appended to these minutes.

If purchased outright, we could get a discount of 14 percent from our usual supplier, APW Computer Supplies, Ltd. This would cause some cash flow difficulties; it might be necessary to obtain extra bank borrowings for these purchases. A loan from the bank would be at 4 percent above bank base rate for any such purchasing. APW Computer Supplies, Ltd. have supplied figures relating to the finance company they use but these were considered too expensive compared to available bank finance.

If the computers were leased, there would be an initial outlay of approximately $80,000 in the first quarter of the budget year. It was felt that this could be absorbed within the current cash flow and no extra financing would be needed. Maintenance contracts have proved expensive and the company would need to consider that it would be paying for maintenance after the first two years of the equipment's life. Under leasing arrangements, our suppliers have offered a service contract throughout the four-year-life of the lease. The disadvantage of the lease is that there is a higher cost, though this may be offset by maintenance bills in later years if the units were purchased.

IT WAS DECIDED that the company would purchase the units needed during the next budget year.

IT WAS DECIDED that the company would arrange with its bankers to provide the additional funds necessary for these purchases.

ACTION. Mark Digby will summarize the exact units needed and the final expenditures. This will be presented to the next meeting.   *Mark Digby*

ACTION. The finance director, Bob Jones, will negotiate an additional loan from Snatchit Bank based on Mr. Digby's expenditures.   *Bob Jones*

Note: We should point out that in reality the example given of a discussion of whether to lease or buy computer equipment would almost certainly not merit such a long report in the minutes and might even be reduced only to decisions and action points. However, the purpose of this example is to show how long tracts of narrative can be made highly readable with some planning and forethought.

Further enhancements

The minutes can be further enhanced by the publication of what we call *long duration* minutes. Some meetings, typically the meeting of a board of school governors, for example, will occasionally produce what is in effect company (or school) policy in discussion. Where a long-term policy has been established, we suggest that at the bottom of the minutes published as set out in our examples is a heading—*Long duration minutes*—and that a synthesized version of the main minutes included in the usual narrative/decision/actions framework should be written out—all italicized. As an example, at the end of our example minutes published as they should be, we might have:

Long duration minutes

The company decided on a policy of purchasing all computer equipment for the foreseeable future.

These long duration minutes might even be moved to a special policy file and circulated separately. All too often committees reinvent the wheel by discussing matters that are already agreed policy and about which they have very little latitude for decision. This can be avoided if people are kept fully up-to-date with current policy.

What Should Be Appended to the Minutes?

We often think of the minutes as a written account of discussion, but a good secretary might do some lateral thinking and recognize that certain items are better presented not in words at all but in other forms.

Reports

As noted in the section on briefing meetings, any reports handed out should be appended to the minutes and a note of their being appended should be added to the main minutes; no synthesis of the reports needs to be included. What should be included in the actual minutes are the discussions or main points arising from the briefing meeting.

Diagrams and statistical charts

Some concepts are better expressed diagrammatically or in statistical groupings and you might ask a presenter to offer you a diagram or chart that you can append to the minutes if he wants points to be made clear to minute readers. You might even consider taking a boring group of statistics to your spreadsheet experts and asking them to express them in, say, a bar chart that you could then append to the minutes. (Do be sure to get the person who presented the information in the first place to check that your bar chart is a proper representation; but nine times out of ten he will be very pleased at your initiative and will think of doing it next time.)

Photographs?

When we presented this concept at a training meeting, we were asked by one delegate, "Do you mean append a photograph of all the people sitting around the table?" Obviously we do not mean that at all! We should also point out that the use of photographs is extremely rare but there are many Brownie points to be had for that creative idea when a photograph is appropriate. We remember a situation when at a meeting one person was torturously trying to describe folds in stressed metals until someone else suggested, "Why don't you try and draw them," and immediately someone else said, "Would it not be better to just photograph them and circulate a photograph." We agree. There are those certain rare times when a photograph really is worth a thousand words and you can save those thousand words by initiating a photograph and circulating it with the minutes. For one or two specified users (the equivalent of those people who have to read the narrative minutes), you might circulate an original print; for most people's use, a photocopy of the photograph will be adequate.

The use of photographs is rare and should not be stretched beyond its sensible limits. However, there are some businesses where circulating a photograph would be perfectly normal (e.g., property development companies, which frequently circulate photographs of sites or buildings for development).

Distribution of Minutes

Minutes should ideally be distributed within 48 hours of the meeting. If minutes are distributed much later, people will often, in the interim, have had discussions on the subjects of the meeting that will have advanced the debate beyond what happened at the meeting. They will then challenge the minutes or ask for them to reflect things that did not happen in the meeting. Many of them will genuinely believe they had these debates in the meeting when in fact they were outside. If the minutes are distributed within 48 hours, people can clearly distinguish between discussions that arose in the meeting and those that arose afterward.

It should also be company policy, and should be encouraged by yourself as much as possible, for people to read the minutes (albeit the 30-second scan of decisions and actions) and feed back to you any comments they have on them as soon as possible.

The Agenda

In this part of the book we have looked at meetings, the secretary's role at meetings, and the published minutes of meetings. The effective running of meetings can only be made possible by the preparation of an informative, purposeful agenda. The aims of the agenda are now detailed.

To confirm the time, date, and place of the forthcoming meeting

The time, date, and place of regular meetings will have been announced on the bottom of the minutes of the previous meeting. Reinforcing this at the top of the agenda confirms the position and also gives the opportunity for change should there be a change of circumstances. However, if the time, date, or place has changed, we would recommend that a covering memo accompanies the agenda, clearly setting out the change, because people are too commonly prone to ignoring the regular details at the top of agendas (even in companies with a good meeting mindset; in companies with a poor meeting attitude, people will probably not even bother to read the agenda until they are sitting in the meeting).

To give members prior warning of what will be discussed at the meeting

When members are given an indication of the subjects to be discussed, they will be able to prepare for their contributions more effectively. This can therefore be likened to a menu.

To guide members through the meeting, indicating subjects that will be discussed in the order in which they will be discussed

As well as being a menu, the agenda should serve as a timetable. For many reasons that will become apparent, when we examine the agenda in detail, people should know roughly the times at which each item will start and end. This will give a planned structure to the meeting and allow the chairperson to make certain decisions about who should be at the meeting, and when.

There is also a psychological component to this. If people making presentations do not know when they are going to be called to give their talk and if they are suddenly called upon by the chairperson to do so, they might become flustered or even panic, and might make a long and rambling, ineffective presentation when with some internal preparation they could have made a shorter but more effective presentation. If a person is to make a presentation in, say, item 6 on the agenda, then she may well be very relaxed during item 4 but during the discussion of item 5—albeit subconsciously—will prepare her body for the presentation. Her breathing will slightly increase, she will force herself to be more alert, and so on. There is a warning here for potential chairpersons; if you decide to move from point 4 straight to point 6, then it would be advisable during the debate on point 4 to alert the people concerned with the presentation of point 6 that you are going to do that and to give them time to psych themselves up; this will make for a more energized and focused presentation, which is to your advantage.

To present a manageable list of items that can be adequately discussed in the time available

As well as a menu and a timetable, what we have in this lesser used function of the agenda is a production target. It is by the recognition of this use of the agenda that meetings can be most easily energized.

In rare cases, companies have an ever-growing list of agenda items that are never discussed. Each agenda has 40 items on it, of which 10 or 12 are always discussed and the rest are carried forward for future discussion (i.e., never). People involved in those discussions become demotivated and certainly never prepare for their presentations, knowing they will not have to make them. In the event that they ever did have to, their unprepared presentations would be ineffective. The production target mentality suggests that rather than debating 12 out of 40 items, a good chairperson should put, say, 15 items on the agenda with a determined effort to debate them all. By increasing the numbers being discussed and keeping people focused on the timetable, the backlog of items will be gradually eliminated. Through the use of production target mentality, such a backlog would never arise again.

More usually in companies, meetings have a finite amount of subjects but an infinite amount of time to discuss them, i.e., the meeting starts at a certain time but finishes when everyone is bored or unconscious, or the school bell rings. A good chairperson should be able to calculate the approximate time needed for a healthy debate on any subject and should structure the meeting accordingly. In most companies, meetings that take three hours can be just as effectively, even more effectively, debated in two and a half hours. Remember that a half hour saved with twenty people around the room is ten staff hours of active work and ten hours spent on things that need to be done rather than ten hours of people in meetings tapping their fingers and asking the question, "Why am I here?"

A good chairperson knows that some ten minutes before the end of any reasonably lengthy discussion is the time when, if that deadline is announced, people will shuffle themselves forward, sit upright, and focus on the debate more strongly.

Therefore if, say, one hour has been allocated for a topic, some ten minutes before the deadline and, having been through all that needs to be discussed, the chairperson announces that there is about ten minutes to go, people will focus on meeting that deadline.

When the agenda is used properly, people will be in meetings only when they are needed, will be constantly aware of deadlines (which will keep them focused and energized) and will learn to make more concise presentations. All of this has a twofold effect: first, in the meeting, people will feel active rather than bored, and this will increase their appreciation of meetings, not least because better decisions will arise; second, outside the meeting, people will have more time to get on with other work rather than feeling that they are being distracted by tedious and boring meetings. The purpose of the effective agenda is to release people from unplanned time into planned time outside the meeting. In other words, the ripple effect of people being in meetings of unknown length is eliminated. The ripple effect arises because a person who is in a meeting but doesn't know when he or she will be coming out will, throughout the day, be sought by other people, who have to leave their offices and put their heads around various doors asking questions like "Is he out yet?"; people waiting to see them or trying to find them will discover that they are not in their offices, and so on *ad infinitum*. When it is clear that a person will be out of a meeting by a certain time, plans for the rest of the day can be made; planned time is worth unplanned time times ten.

Distribution of Agendas

Agendas and attachments should be distributed one week before the meeting. It should be company policy that attached reports, briefing papers, and previous minutes must be read before the meeting. If the company culture is weak, then it may be appropriate to distribute a reminder of the meeting two days before the meeting, but this should never be allowed to become a habit and after a few such reminders it should be announced that there will in the future be no further reminders, and that the agenda will serve as the only notification.

Agendas: How Not to Do It

Note that references to "routine" and "nonroutine" are notes for you as reader (explained below) and would not appear on the published agenda.

Tiger Moth, Ltd.

Agenda

The Agenda of the meeting of the Planning Committee to be held in Room 7 at 10 A.M. on Friday January 13, 199–.

To be present:
A. Johnson (Chairman)
I. M. Biggles (Secretary)
R. Hoven
P. Pilot
Y. Knott

1. Apologies for absence.
2. Minutes of last meeting.
3. Matters arising.
4. Report of the finance committee (routine).
5. Report of the catering sub-committee (routine).
6. Report re Chocks Away, Ltd. takeover (nonroutine).
7. Report re company stationery (nonroutine).
8. Any other business.
9. Date, time, place of next meeting.

Agendas: How to Do It

Super Space Shuttle, Ltd

Agenda

Agenda of the meeting of the Planning Committee. To be held in Meeting Room 7 from 10 A.M. to 2 P.M. on Friday September 13, 199–.

To be present:
D. Dare (Chairman)
B. Rogers (Secretary)
F. Gordon
Barbara Eller
T. Tinn (from 1:20 P.M. to 1:45 P.M.)
J. Verne (from 11:30 A.M. to 1:20 P.M.)

1. Apologies for absence.
2. Minutes of the last meeting. [10 mins]
3. Matters arising. [20 mins]
4. Report of the finance committee (routine). [30 mins]
5. Report of the catering subcommittee (routine). [30 mins]
   (In the real agenda this may consit of several items, each
   with its own time allocation. Very little description is likely to
   be needed because of the routing nature of the items.)
6. Report re Chocks Away, Ltd. takeover (nonroutine). [110 mins]
   (Descriptive paragraph detailing purpose of discussion
   and desired outcome, decision, recommendation etc.
   All attendees should be briefed in this paragraph as to what
   is expected of them.)
7. Report re company stationery (nonroutine). [25 mins]
   (Descriptive paragraph detailing purpose of discussion
   and desired outcome, decision, recommendations, etc.
   All attendees should be briefed in this paragraph as to what
   is expected of them.)
8. Any other business (AOB). [10 mins]
9. Date, time, place of next meeting. [5 mins]

The differences between the two are similar to the differences between the Tiger Moth (TM) and the Space Shuttle (SS).

Notification of time, date, and place

Important in our agenda is the announcement not only of a starting time but also of a finishing time. This, as we have said, enables people to plan the rest of their day and also allows those planning the meeting to timetable and target the discussion at the meeting.

To be present

There is always going to be a core of people who are required at the meeting throughout, but there are also a lot of people who can be invited for specific items of discussion and who therefore are free to do productive work when they are not needed in the meeting and, by not being in a meeting, are prevented from chipping in irrelevant comments based on the need to justify their being there, which unnecessarily lengthens debates in which they are not involved.

Apologies for absence

Make note of those who were expected to be at the meeting but who have been unable to be there. This is a good time to remind the secretary that if some people cannot be at the meeting, the secretary should make sure that their presence was not essential to particular discussions, that would otherwise have to be cancelled. It may even be that people who have been invited for specific topics can be told not to attend as that topic will have to be carried forward in the absence of particular people. Obviously, tight agendas do place a responsibility on people to report to the secretary as early as possible if they know they are not able to attend a meeting; it also places on them a responsibility to attend meetings whenever possible rather than to treat them as something to do if they have nothing better on!

Minutes of the last meeting

People should have already read the minutes of the last meeting, which were circulated 48 hours after the meeting itself. We have seen some meetings where between 45 minutes and an hour is allocated for this in order to give people time to sit down and read the minutes in the meeting. This is very boring and nonproductive and starts the meeting off with very low energy, setting a bad pattern. Everyone has some spare time (on trains, in the bath, whatever) in which to read the minutes and therefore on the agenda this item should only be for picking up points rising from the previously read minutes. No more than ten minutes should ever be necessary if the minutes were prepared well in the first place.

Matters arising

Matters arising should not be an excuse to redebate those matters that have already been debated in previous meetings and therefore we would recommend no more than five minutes per topic, picking up the action points of previous meetings where they do not apply to major topics of discussion in this meeting. Matters arising should amount to quick reports based on activity rather than lengthy discussions. If a lengthy discussion is required based on something that has already been discussed, the topic should be placed on a new agenda under its own topic heading.

Routine business

There are always a number of routine items that arise in every meeting, such as reports of finance committees and reports of the canteen committee. Because these reports are regular and usually run through a regular format, we would recommend that those responsible for the reports should prepare them in written form and send them to the secretary, who can circulate them with the agenda. Therefore, only a short amount of time is needed on the agenda, to discuss points arising from the report rather than to go through the report in laborious detail.

Nonroutine items

On the agenda we have included items referring to the Chocks Away, Ltd. takeover and company stationery. Because these are nonroutine, i.e., they do not recur, people will not be aware of what is expected of them unless the agenda makes this clear. This is where the agenda becomes an important briefing document. It should not be a crib sheet simply setting out the heading from which people can draw their own expectations. Rather it should be a descriptive paragraph detailing the purpose of the discussion and the desired outcome, i.e., whether a decision or recommendation is needed or whether an action will be required. All attendees should be briefed in each paragraph relating to a nonroutine item as to what is expected of them. This will enable them to fully prepare for their contribution. If a decision is needed, then there will be no excuse for anyone turning up and commenting, "Oh, I didn't know we had to have the facts today; I thought we were only reviewing matters" or something similar. If a decision is needed, then people will be expected to produce any facts or figures that are required at that meeting.

There is no recommended length to the description given of what is required on nonroutine items although obviously it should be as short and concise as possible. It may run to several paragraphs (unusual in British agendas) or it may even be a page in its own right that is referred to from the main agenda. By reading it, people will understand exactly what they are expected to offer to the meeting discussion on that point. This will also enable the meeting to run in a more energized way and to a more effective timetable.

Any other business

There are some agendas that have very little other than apologies for absence, minutes of the last meeting, matters arising, and any other business. Clearly this is the least planned type of agenda and is a virtual invitation for rambling long-winded poor discussions. On the other hand, there are some businesses that absolutely forbid any other business on the grounds that unplanned discussion is worthless. However, we must recognize that there will always be one or two items for discussion that will arise after the preparation of the agenda and before the meeting. Any other business therefore has its proper place if it is properly planned.

The solution is to recognize the situation and allow for any other business no more than, say, ten minutes. The logic of this is that if an item that needs to be discussed arises after the preparation of the agenda but before the meeting and if it can be debated and polished off in five minutes, i.e., it is urgent but does not have lengthy ramifications, then by all means do it and get rid of it so it doesn't have to appear on the agenda again. However, if any topic for discussion is going to take more than a few minutes, then it probably has ramifications and complications and time will be wasted debating it under "Any other business" because after the meeting people will reflect on the debate and bring out all the arguments they would have prepared for it if they had been given time to prepare. In short, you will find it reappearing on the agenda again at a later meeting and it will have to be redebated; the time spent debating it under "Any other business" will have been wasted.

Date, time, and place of next meeting

This is your opportunity to announce the next meeting or regular sequences of meetings, but do not forget that the date, time, and place are also announced on the agenda of that meeting, where you can notify changes to the plan if necessary (see notes relating to the agenda earlier).

Exercise 3 – Agenda design and publication

Points for discussion in the meeting:

- Whether we can produce "Bumpers 2," our new bumper car project, for a new fairground chain by the end of the month. (Note for delegates: this will depend on whether we can get the X1 machine on-line or we might have to use the slower X2 machine, with overtime.)
- To coordinate overtime schedules with the workforce.
- To coordinate new overtime rates with the union representative.
- The maintenance schedules on the X1 and X2 machines.
- To confirm the installation of the new RAF (random access filing) system.
- The routine report of the finance subcommittee.
- The routine report of the cafeteria usage committee.

Required

Produce an agenda for the meeting. Be creative: where information you feel you need is missing, make it up (but be ready to justify it).

A model answer

AGENDA: Meeting of the XYZ Production Committee.
Date: March 12, 1992. Time: from 10 A.M. to 2 P.M.
Venue: Room 7, Conference Block, Witney site.

Those to be present:
Miss Susan Scarlett (Chair)
Mrs. Snowe White (Secretary)
Professor Bob Plumb
Colonel Colman Mustard
Mr. Gann Green (filing department) from 11:15 A.M. to 12 noon
Mrs. P. Cox (filing department) from 11:15 A.M. to 12 noon
John Waddington (union representative) from 12 noon to end

1.	Apologies for absence.	5 mins
2.	Minutes of the last meeting.	5 mins

3. Matters arising.   15 mins

4. Report of the finance subcommittee.   30 mins

5. Report of the cafeteria usage subcommittee. (Note: there will be discussion of whether to include hot foods on the menu for the first time. A decision will be required so that the cafeteria can place orders for the next month.)   25 mins

6. To confirm installation of the new filing system. We will have a report from those who have been pilot-running the plan followed by our agreement to turn over the whole admin section to the system, or to abandon its use.   30 mins

(Note: You might plan a short break here, not noted on the agenda—don't encourage people to have their secretaries bring messages to the meeting room at this time.)

7. To coordinate the new overtime rates with the union representative.   1 hour

8. List of maintenance schedules on the X1 and X2 machines.   20 mins

9. To coordinate overtime schedules with the workforce.   15 mins

10. To decide whether we can produce "Bumpers 2," our new bumper car project, for a new fairground chain by the end of the month.   30 mins

11. Any other business.   5 mins

12. Date, time, and place of next meeting.

Notes to the model answer

Many of the points raised by the example are explained in the section on agendas. One point comes through this example most clearly, however. There must be a logical order to items on agendas to prevent time being wasted in debates on things we can do nothing about. Item 10—to decide to produce Bumpers 2—could not have been debated successfully if we had not already discussed and agreed on items 7, 8, and 9. If we do not know whether we have the machines and the labor force to do the job, we might be wasting our time to discuss our preferences on item 10.

PART 2

Advanced Telephone
Techniques

The Telephone Problem

Communication studies indicate that we remember:

- 10 percent of what we hear;
- 40 percent of what we hear and see;
- 70 percent of what we hear, see, and do.

The best teachers and trainers know this and arrange their presentations to be most memorable by combining "hear, see, and do" in their delivery. In addition to standing in front of their delegates and talking to them, they use visual aids, such as overhead projected slides, diagrams, bullet points drawn up on the flip charts, and so on. They involve their delegates interactively in processes where the delegates work through problems and find solutions, discovering main points for themselves, usually in small workshop groups where they can interact with each other as well as with the trainer.

The telephone problem is obvious: at face value a telephone appears only to allow the people on the call to hear each other, leaving the possibility of only 10 percent of the call's information being retained in memory. There are, however, a number of techniques that bridge the gap between the spoken word and fully interactive presentations. If you apply these when using the telephone, you will increase the impact of your message.

Do not try to describe obviously visual images, such as a view of a building or the blueprint of a product, over the telephone. It will be virtually impossible for the receiver to recreate the correct image of what you are describing. Similarly, do not read out long lists of statistics or repetitive details over the telephone; this will bore the listener, who will not be able to absorb what you are saying. If you have to communicate such information, combine the telephone with—using a little forethought—either the mailed or facsimile transmission. Send drawings or diagrams, copies of photographs, long lists of statistics, and so on either through the mail or over the fax to your recipient and then follow up with a phone call, first making sure that he or she has looked at your visual presentation and had the opportunity to absorb the details. When telephoning the recipient, make sure that you have a copy of the information you have sent, so that you can refer specifically to what he or she is looking at. (And make sure that recipients have the papers in front of them when you call by asking them to do so and by indicating that you will be highlighting specific points that they might want to look at or jot down notes against.)

By making the telephone call as interactive as possible, you also force the recipient of the call to move from *hear* and *see* to *do*. When you have said something to the recipient and she has acknowledged it (with a yes or a grunt), ask her to confirm exactly what you said. When you have given her a telephone number, ask her to read it back to you. These techniques ensure that the person must be writing down the main points you want her to note. This is where you are forcing her attention to a more interactive level of listening.

Finally, KISS, or Keep It Short and Simple. The telephone is not a medium that is highly effective for information flow and retention over long periods and you are best advised to keep your information concise and short and to the point. Together with the use of visual images and checking back, a short, high-impact telephone call increases the amount of impact you make and the retention of your message in the mind of the recipient.

Exercise 4

Test your ability to transmit a visual image in words alone. Put a visual image on the desk in front of you, perhaps a painting, a reasonably complex diagram, or one of Escher's famous optical illusions, and describe it to a friend over the telephone, asking her to draw what you are describing. When you are next together, compare the original with the drawing. In the vast majority of cases, there will be many differences between the two and in a smaller percentage of cases, barely any resemblance between them.

Exercise 5

Repeat the above exercise, but describing to someone the room you are sitting in, asking him or her to sketch a floor plan from your description. Again, compare the two. (The problem with this form of communication is that we all carry prejudicial images in our mind and, when the information is not specifically given, recipients draw from their own belief what they think they are hearing, creating the missing bits in their own mind. As a simple example, you might describe a filing cabinet in the corner of the room and the person will draw a four-drawer filing cabinet, which is by far the most common type, when you meant a two-drawer filing cabinet.)

In the James Bond film *Thunderball*, Agent 007 is on the telephone in a health clinic, describing to his secretary in her office in London a symbol he has seen on an enemy agent's wrist. We have previously seen the symbol in the film and we are able to watch his secretary draw the symbol as he describes it. The symbol is shown in Figure 5. His secretary draws virtually exactly the same symbol from 007's description of "a red square with a spike through it." We have tested this in interactive training and so far have 17 quite different images based on that simple description!

Figure 5 What would others draw if you described this to them verbally?

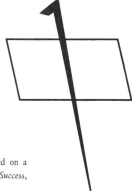

NOTE: This technique of telephone visualization is based on a process used in the British Telecom booklet *The Language of Success*, published by British Telecom plc in 1991.

Your Telephone Image

Behavior is the only part of us that is visible to others. It is important to remember this. No matter what we think, what we feel, what beliefs we hold true, and so on, the way we behave (consciously or subconsciously) is the only part of us that allows other people to interpret those inner feelings. From our behavior, people will create their mental image of us.

Telephone Behavior is verbal. How does this affect our manner on the telephone?

Formal dress versus casual dress

For some secretaries, the choice of dress is dictated by many factors other than the telephone. They may be involved interactively with clients and need to dress appropriately or, quite simply, they may be at the reception desk where they are receiving not only telephone calls but also visitors. Their dress code will be dictated by company policy as much as their own inner feelings. However, some secretaries remain within their own offices, and their only contact with clients is over the telephone. They appear to have a choice: should they dress formally or casually? Does it matter if the secretary who is only dealing with people over the telephone dresses in jeans and a T-shirt rather than a neat skirt or pants and blouse, or suit and tie?

Certainly there are some telephone training courses that point out that because the person cannot see you, you are at liberty to dress in any way you want to. We could not disagree more strongly!

The way we dress indicates something of our attitude toward the work we are doing. If formal dress would normally be expected of us in our interactive relationship with clients, then formal dress is appropriate if we are using the telephone to speak to those clients. It sets out something of our own attitude toward the work we are doing. Therefore, while the way we dress might not directly affect the way we speak to people over the telephone, the attitude that allows us to dress casually when formal dress would normally be expected also allows us to act casually when more formal behavior would be more appropriate. Many years ago, one of the authors of this book learned that very clearly: working from an office in his home at the time, he would often only dress in suit and tie on days when he had appointments with clients, dressing casually on other days when he would be working alone at his desk. This was a business that involved many phone calls during the day with clients and others. One friend often played a game with him: when he and his friend spoke on the telephone, the friend tried to guess whether he was formally or casually dressed. The hit rate was extraordinarily high! This was a clear lesson that to act appropriately toward clients, he should dress as neatly when speaking to clients over the telephone as he would if he was meeting them in person.

There are exceptions. Certain companies and certain individuals understand that the appropriate dress for their clients is casual (most typically those involved in artistic expressions, such as designers, some computer software producers, some creative advertising personnel). They should continue to dress as they would when meeting clients, which is often very much more casual than, say, the dress of solicitors and accountants. Dress code is something like jargon: it states the category in which we work as well as our attitude toward it.

Use of Standard English or use of slang

Standard English does not mean speaking in the Edwardian style of a monarch talking to his or her subjects, or that curious voice of the BBC of the 1950s ("This is the BBC calling the World from London"). Standard English can be friendly and conversational. Standard English is suggested for telephone behavior as it is considerate of others. Slang is a form of jargon in that it communicates meaning only between those who understand such minority expressions. As such slang is offensive, in that, first, it suggests membership of a club that the recipient who does not understand it is not a member of and, second, it shows that you are more concerned with using your own expressions than considering the needs of others. Appropriate telephone behavior shows your consideration of others.

For example, one British credit controller talking on the telephone to a colleague in another office in another part of the country referred to one absconding debtor he could not locate by saying: "He has had it away on his toes." Such an expression might properly indicate to someone—most traditionally in the East End of London— that the person had run away to avoid detection. It might have been very unclear to someone from another background.

A willingness to help or wanting the caller to go away

Because of the pressure on some receptionists, they are actually instructed by their department heads to "process" calls as quickly as possible. Their job is to get people off the main switchboard and to their destination as quickly as possible, not for the positive reason of wanting to be efficient to the customer but for the somewhat negative reason of so-called efficiency for themselves. This usually translates as meaning that the company is not prepared to employ enough receptionists to take care of its clients' needs and the clients are being asked to pay for that by being treated badly. If you think that your job is to get this caller off the phone so that you can get on with the next one, then you will transmit that very clearly to your caller. You will be telling that person that you are thinking, "What can I do to get rid of this caller?"

Willingness to help is the appropriate telephone language for building relationships with clients; it starts at the reception desk and goes all the way through a telephone call to secretaries, executive assistants, and bosses. Willingness to help is categorized by behaving as if the question in your mind is, "What can I do to help this person?" This leads to the relationship that you should be generating between yourself and the person on the other end of the telephone.

Telephone Relationships

As soon as the telephone rings and you are reaching for it, you know you are about to enter into a relationship with someone for a brief period of time. What should that relationship be?

Exercise 6

Consider that you are expecting welcome guests at your house one evening, either for coffee or for dinner. Jot down a note of the things that you will do when they arrive.

We hope you will have noted some of the following:

- You seek to make them welcome by the things you say, your body language, and the things you do for them.
- You seek to make them comfortable by taking their coats, giving them a comfortable place to sit, offering them things such as a warm drink if it is cold outside, and so on.
- You offer them things such as drinks and light snacks, or perhaps offer to dry their wet outer clothing if they have come in from the rain.

- You seek to deal with their needs as well as their wants. You might know, for example, that they will be more comfortable if they have the opportunity to telephone their partner or their parents to let them know they have arrived safely, and you offer them the opportunity to do that in case they feel embarrassed to ask. When they are leaving, particularly for a long journey back to their own home, you might remind them that they are welcome to use the bathroom facilities to freshen up.

- You try to find ways to solve their problems. If, for example, they are unsure how they are going to get to a train station to catch their return train home, you might offer to drive them to the station or to find an appropriate taxi telephone number and book one for them.

- You make them feel of value. You offer them conversation that you feel is interesting and that you hope they will feel equally interested in, and, even more importantly, you listen to their conversation knowing it is of interest to them and being glad that they want to share it with you.

- You make them feel that they are doing you a favor and being generous by calling on you. And you go out of your way to make sure that people do not feel they are imposing on you.

- You feel disappointed if they don't return the evening, i.e., inviting you to their home for a meal. The disappointment is based on a possibility that you have failed to act as a good host.

How do we translate this into our telephone relationship?

We start by recognizing that as we pick up the telephone we are entering into a partnership with the caller, rather than a "two-sides-of-the-fence" struggle. Both parties want the caller to be speaking to the right person. At the front desk particularly, this means taking the time and trouble to make sure that you understand the caller's needs in order to put her through to the right person rather than shunting her through to the first person who comes to mind, only to be passing her on to a series of calls, with many people saying "Oh, you don't want me, you want such and such, please wait while I transfer you."

During the course of your working week, take a note of how many receptionists clearly do not present the attitude of relationship (or welcome guest) to their callers. Both authors of this book have certainly found an increasing tendency for receptionists to listen to half a request and not even bother to interrupt, but merely to cut off the call and put it through to someone, usually the wrong person. And receptionists seem quite unconcerned about this in many companies. In one case, one of the authors telephoned a company, quoting a reference as requested, but was cut off halfway through the reference without a word from the receptionist and put through to a completely wrong department. It turned out that the whole reference was required in order to determine the appropriate department. With this book in mind, the author retelephoned the company to speak to the same receptionist and asked her why she had acted so inappropriately. Her reply was, "I've got a load of calls coming through here and I can't waste time talking to everybody. The people I've put you through to are on the same floor; they could have transferred you to the right people without all this fuss, couldn't they?"

You want to be more than your caller expects or hopes for, not less. If you receive a telephone call from someone who does not know which department he wants to speak to and has no reference or extension number to offer you, then do not take a lucky guess with the all too often heard words, "I'll put you through to so and so, they might be able to help you" (i.e., "What can I do to get rid of this person?"), but ask the person some brief questions about his problem so that you can begin to identify the department or person in your company that is genuinely best able to offer assistance (i.e., "What can I do to help this person?"). A word of caution is needed here: do not make the caller give you all the details of his inquiry believing that you can answer the question, or he will only have to repeat the whole thing again to the person you put him through to. Explain to him clearly that you are asking only in order to identify the proper person to put him through to, and ask him to give you a brief outline of the problem. He will then not feel that he is having constantly to repeat his problem in the hope of finding someone who can deal with it.

The Telephone Army

There are many different types of people on the telephone. We have divided them into five categories.

The "yes" brigade

The "yes" brigade always say "yes," always agree with you, always promise things, but probably don't act on your call.

To deal with them, ask questions that challenge their understanding, to make sure that they cannot just be saying "yes" while doing and thinking nothing about the points. Commit them to dates and times when they will confirm they have done the actions they promise. Make a point of always telephoning back and challenging people who have made you promises and haven't met them, so that next time they will know that you are the sort of person that they will either have to be honest with from the start or be challenged by in the future. In some cases it may be appropriate to follow up the telephone call by a fax message confirming to them what they have promised; once seen in stark black-and-white writing, the promises seem somehow more solid and requiring of commitment.

The conscientious objectors

The conscientious objectors will say "no" to almost anything out of habit. They are very depressing to talk to. To deal with them, be positive and enthusiastic. Do not take no for an answer but don't get into arguments with them or they will dig in their heels. At any positive signs, act very warmly and encourage their interaction.

The know-it-all contingent

Characteristically, these people have loud mouths, are barnstorming, and never admit they are wrong. They rarely listen to you even if you get a word in. To deal with them, try not to challenge their perceived self-image of their importance or their expertise. Have your own facts at hand. It may sometimes help to make them feel important in order to get a short-term positive response. Do not, however, compromise your own assertive beliefs in yourself. Use permission questioning such as, "Could I suggest that we do such and such?" This adds to a feeling of building something between yourselves that will make the person feel all the more involved in the solution you are attempting to generate.

The secret service

The secret service is like talking to a sponge: all you ever hear are "uhms" and "ahs" and you never really know what they are thinking. To deal with them, demand responses and leave silences that they have to fill in (later we will examine the benefits of silence in telephone calls).

The terrorists

These people are not openly aggressive but shoot from behind cover. They use innuendo and sarcasm. To deal with them, you need to be subtle. Do not react with sarcasm of your own and never acknowledge innuendo. You do not have to accept their offered version of events but challenge assertively with facts of your own. Break down their hostility with your own calmness and dignity.

The Mechanics

Part of a good telephone manner is to be aware of the practical, mechanical rules of telephone equipment.

Know the machinery

Take the time and trouble—and perhaps a training course—to understand fully the capabilities of your telephone system. Whenever your phones are upgraded, learn how to transfer calls rather than lose callers when trying to do so, forcing them to ring back again. Learn how to put callers on hold. And learn the difference between internal and external calls if the new system has a way of ringing differently in each case.

How long should you leave the telephone or extensions ringing?

Make it a rule never to allow telephones to ring more than three to five times before you answer them. From the caller's perspective, five rings is a long time and quickly becomes irritating.

If an extension is not answered, what do you do?

Transfer the call back yourself rather than leaving it ringing, explain to the caller that you are personally taking care of her, apologize for the delay, and explain that you are looking for an alternative person who can assist her. If appropriate, offer to take a note of her name and telephone number (and some other details indicated on the message pad design later in this part) and assure her that you will be responsible for getting a message to the appropriate person, asking him to ring her back. This will save an unnecessarily protracted phone call waiting while you locate a person, which, if nothing else, will save the cost of the phone call.

How often do you go back to a caller on hold?

Do not leave a person on hold for more than 30 seconds before going back and apologizing for the fact that he is having to continue to hold. At appropriate intervals, also ask if he wishes to continue the call or would prefer for you to take a message and arrange for someone to call him back.

Exercise 7

Ask a friend to sit with you in a room. Out of his eye range, place within your view a wristwatch with a second hand. Say to your friend, "There's something I must tell you." And then say nothing while discreetly watching the seconds passing on the watch. See how long it is before he breaks your silence by asking you something like "What's wrong?" or some other question regarding your silence. It will probably be no more than five to ten seconds. This gives some measure of the time before a silent pause can become irritating or at least of concern.

Exercise 8

Repeat the same situation with a person in the room with you but simply ask her to remain silent for a moment or two. Out of her eye range, wait for 30 seconds on your watch and then ask her how long he or she thinks the silence was. In training room tests, the average response is between 45 seconds and one minute; we have even had suggestions of over two minutes. This indicates that 30 seconds can be a long time in a person's mind.

Know alternative people you can put a caller through to

One of the authors of this book called a large international company asking for one of its senior staff members. The receptionist had sufficient information in front of her to be able to say "Anna—is not in the office today. Can someone else help you?" This author was happy to be put through to an alternative person who could take the call and said so, but the receptionist then responded by saying, "Can you tell me which department she works for? I can't put you through unless I know who to put you through to."

The receptionist should know the location of staff in her offices, possibly with a cross-referenced telephone list on her desk, and certainly in the case of senior staff (and particularly where she had obviously been given a note that that person was not in the office that day) should have to hand the number of the person who could take her calls or deal with questions to her department. To have located such information as soon as the receptionist knew that that person was absent from the office would have shown an intention to be considerate to callers, an attitude that reflects the proper relationship.

Announce people before putting them through

Remember to tell the receiver if the caller wanted someone else and he is being offered as an alternative. This will prevent, first, the caller having to repeat her whole message to the next person if you have prebriefed him and, second, the receiver of the call from saying something like "Oh no, you don't want me, you want so and so (the person whom he has already been told is not in the office and for whom the person now taking the call as the fielded substitute)."

Consider the needs of people at pay phones

Be brief because the caller's time is not only literally money, but probably money that is quickly running out. Get the message down quickly. Take the pay phone number if possible, but be aware that many pay phones do not allow incoming calls.

Offer to phone the caller back if practical. (If the caller is using a calling card, these courtesies would be unnecessary.)

Consider the needs of people telephoning from someone else's office

First, offer to phone him back as this will save the client he is with from paying for the telephone call. Remember to get not only the telephone number but also the extension and a note of the person he is with at that time in case you have to get back to him through a receptionist. Remember to ask your caller to clear it with the client he is with and the switchboard to put you through when you call back, or there is the danger that you will be told by the receptionist, "I'm sorry, he is in a meeting with so and so (your boss, perhaps) and can't be interrupted."

People phoning from hotels or conferences

Remember to take as much information relating to room numbers, extension numbers, and so on as you can, so that you can track them down. Remember that the receptionist will probably have very little idea of the exact whereabouts of people in the hotel, let alone a conference.

Pick up the telephone in the hand you do not write with

This may be obvious, but it allows you immediately to begin jotting down a message or details of the call in order to keep it in mind.

Place a pad and pencil beside each telephone

All telephone calls have the potential to require some kind of note to be taken. Make sure that you do not have to keep the caller holding on while you search around the office trying to find something on which to write notes.

Keep a pad and pencil with you

If your office is not efficient enough to supply pads and pencils by its telephones, or if there is a bad habit in your office of people taking the pad and pencil and moving them elsewhere, then get into the habit of carrying a small pad and pencil in a pocket so that you can always jot down points from telephone calls.

Structure messages

Below we provide a recommended message pad, covering the following points.

- Who called?

- Of what company (company address)?
- What is the caller's telephone number and extension?
- Who was the caller asking for?
- What date and time was the call?
- Who took the call?
- Is it urgent or nonurgent?
- Does the caller want to be called, or will she call back?
- Make sure that there is a clear, brief, message clearly written out.
- Check all the details with the caller to make sure you have not made any mistakes.
- If any action has been taken as a result of the phone call, make sure that that is noted on the message pad for the receiver to read. (When delivering the message to the person it is destined for, you might consider taking the appropriate files out of the filing cabinet and handing them over with the message, so that the recipient of the message is fully able to review what work has been done before telephoning back to the caller.)
- Make sure that messages not yet distributed to people are handed over to new receptionists on shift changes.

Message pad design

Telephone message

For: Caller:
Date: Company name:
Time: Telephone No: Ext:
                               Company address:

Urgent / nonurgent

Taken by:

Voice mail: yes/no
               time recorded

Message:

Answering the Telephone

There are some basic rules for appropriate answering of the telephone.

- Answer promptly. As already stated, no telephone should ring more than three to five times.
- For external calls, give the name of the company and say, "Good morning" or "Good afternoon." You should offer them either your name or the name of your department in order to confirm to them that they are speaking to the right person.
- Internal calls. When picking up the telephone, give the department name and your own name.
- Do not rely on memory; write things down.
- Thank the caller for telephoning, confirming your guest-host relationship with the caller, in that she was welcome.
- Do anything you have promised to do.

Create an Identity for Yourself

When answering a call use your own name, e.g., "XYZ Department, Mary Smith speaking, how may I help you?" By doing this, you will also establish your own identity within your company. It does mean that you will then take ownership of the call as people will identify with you directly. Use this to your advantage and become known for your helpfulness.

Ways of Listening

There are three levels of telephone listening: passive listening, surface listening, and active listening. With telephone conversations, only active listening is valid. The one-to-one situation and the need to replace body language and eye contact mean that in order to get the most from a telephone conversation both parties must be active and involved throughout.

Passive listening

The passive listener fakes attention rather than being genuinely interested. She makes the occasional grunt, "yes" or acknowledgment merely to indicate to the person at the other end of the line that she is still there but if challenged often has not heard what is being said and certainly has not comprehended it. The passive listener occasionally hears something that is of interest to her and tunes in to the conversation only to wait for a chance to have her say without real concern for what the other person is saying. Once she has had her say, she tunes out of the conversation and continues to listen only in spurts. The passive listener is very often doing something else while holding the telephone to her ear (typically, reading, opening letters, rearranging the desk).

Surface listening

The surface listener is not as distracted as the passive listener and is at a low level tuned into the conversation throughout. However, the person is often hearing but not comprehending and failing to understand the nuances or subtleties of the message being given to him. The surface listener remains emotionally detached. Surface listening is characterized by the lack of interaction between the two people in the telephone conversation; the surface listener absorbs what is being said at a low level but does not react, comment, add to, or drive the conversation in any way. The surface listener will often agree to what he is being asked to do but not having thought through his own commitments, will often not do what he has said he will. The surface listener often does not take notes, leading to a lack of follow-up on his part.

Active listening (the right way to listen)

The active listener is involved in the conversation, commenting on what she is hearing, adding to it and occasionally changing the direction of the conversation as both parties drive it forward. The active listener is absorbed in what is being said to her and understands it at an emotional level, picking up nuances and underlying meanings. The active listener is interactive, using paraphrase and feedback; in other words, she will absorb something that has been heard and paraphrase that, feeding it back to the person who said it in order to be certain she has understood exactly what is meant. If she has misunderstood it, she is ready and willing to listen to the corrected version. The active listener occasionally takes notes of items for follow-up or matters to be put on file and will read the note back with the person to make sure it is correct and valid. The active listener will, when being asked to make a commitment (to make another telephone call, to call back, to do some other act), consider carefully her work schedule and confirm or renegotiate requests. Having made the commitment, she is the most likely of telephone users actually to fulfill and meet those commitments.

Barriers to Active Listening

Even the best users of telephones are up against their own human qualities when trying to be active listeners.

The brain works more quickly than people can speak

Active listeners absorb what is being said to them and in doing so are thinking ahead to their responses and the wider implications of what is being said, and may be creating images in their minds of alternative scenarios that will arise on the basis of what they are hearing. As they become involved in this imagery, which is essential for the effective understanding of complex parts of the conversation, so their listening level will drop and they may fail to pick up on what is being said to them after whatever it was that started them creating images in the first place.

The solution to this is either to feel free to describe that series of images and share them with the speaker, which carries both parties along at the same pace or, if that is not desirable or practical, to indicate to the speaker that you wish to take some notes down and ask him to slow down for a few moments. No notes might need to be taken, but the listener may use that time to absorb the implications of what she is hearing before acknowledging to the other person in the conversation that he should continue. Active listeners going through this process may be doodling on paper in front of them; this is not the doodle of bored people distracting themselves from a conversation they are not involved in, but usually a visual or diagrammatic way of assisting themselves in working out their own images.

You cannot do two things at once

Some people seem to downgrade the telephone to the point where, because they cannot be seen by the person they are speaking to, they believe they can do many other things at the same time. The list is endless: reading the sports pages, applying makeup or doing their nails, opening the mail, rearranging their desk, mouthing instructions to other members of their staff or office. The most efficient person does not distract himself during a telephone conversation, but by being an active and involved participant in the conversation produces a quicker and better result and frees himself from unnecessary subsequent telephone calls, leaving himself more time free to do the other things. In the end, active listening is more efficient; it is certainly more appreciated by the person speaking to you.

Strong emotion blots out comprehension

If you are extremely emotional, you tend not to absorb the words and descriptions being given to you, though you may well pick up the general meanings. For example, someone who is told of the death of a very close friend or relative on the telephone will often come away from the telephone call fully understanding what has happened but then find she has to call back for specific details such as names of hospitals or telephone numbers, or, if she has written them down, will find that when she reads her own notes a few minutes later they seem almost like something written by someone else. In a business situation, the classic mistake to avoid is to make a complaint as soon as you have discovered that you have something to complain about. Often you are poorly prepared for the call, let alone the possibility that you have misunderstood what has happened. In any situation where strong emotions are involved, allow yourself time to absorb as much as you can beforehand, which will increase your ability to pay attention to the detail of the call.

Never listen dismissively

It is a natural tendency of people to form opinions at the earliest possible stage. This is part of our survivalist mind: when faced with any situation we make judgments in order to determine whether it holds a threat to us. However, if we are unaware of this and we form prejudicial strong opinions before all the facts are known, it is often difficult to change those opinions when other facts are presented. As far as possible, try not to be judgmental or dismissive until you are certain that you have all the facts necessary to form an opinion.

Interpreting What You Hear

Deprived of eye contact and body language, you depend on what clues you can pick up in tone of voice and the words spoken to interpret the more subtle meanings of what is being said to you.

Listen to the tone of voice

Does the tone of voice indicate that the person is concerned, worried, demanding, on solid ground, on unsure ground? Often there will be inconsistency between the words being spoken (which may appear to be very certain) and the tone of voice (which indicates the opposite). Inconsistency in the tone of voice compared to the words being spoken usually indicates that the person speaking to you is testing you for your reactions or opinions.

Consider why humor is being used

Genuine humor is easy to identify: it arises interactively between the two of you and has meaning because it builds a bridge between you in an area where you share feelings or knowledge. However, humor is often used inappropriately and although this is also easy to identify, the reasons for it are perhaps less clear. Inappropriate humor may be used to hide the fact that the person speaking believes she is on unsure ground, or a person may use humor to ingratiate herself with you. Most classically, salespeople will try to use humor to soften you up for a sales pitch.

Pauses, stutters, hesitations, and repetitions

We rely on our intuition to tell us whether a pause is genuine or not. A genuine pause will arise where a person is taking time to be certain that he expresses concern for you in the way he describes his requirements. However, an inappropriate pause may indicate that something is being held back from you (possibly a truth or something that would expose a lie), and you might consider why you are not being given a fuller picture.

Stutters and hesitations (other than the genuine difficulties of those with speech disabilities) usually indicate that the person is seeking to manipulate you or your opinions in some way and is uncertain how you will receive her view of the world or what she wants you to do. Stutters and hesitations of this nature should put you on your guard because they suggest that the person speaking has already identified your probable objections and hopes that you will not voice them. Take your time to think through what is being asked of you.

Repetitions usually arise because the person speaking is unsure whether he is making a point with sufficient impact. This may represent insecurity on his part, but usually indicates that you are not being interactive. Perhaps you have dropped out of active listening and are now surface or passively listening, and this has been identified by the speaker, who is seeking to make sure that you understand what is being said to you.

Slips of the tongue

It is believed by many that slips of the tongue often reveal what is genuinely being thought by the person speaking. Because the brain works faster than we can speak, we sometimes find that we have said what we have thought about before we have realized its implications. Sometimes what we say is to hide what we really think, but we can't stop thinking it and sometimes it slips out. A mistake of a con man, for example, might be to misspeak the phrase "Things to do and people to see" as "Things to see and people to do."

Physical posture

The tone of voice will often indicate the physical posture of the speaker even though you cannot see her. One friend of ours (the one who could tell if the person speaking to him on the telephone was formally dressed or otherwise) could also tell whether or not the person he was speaking to was sitting up in a chair or leaning back with his feet on the table. The tone of voice being produced by the physical posture may indicate relaxation, tension, concern, lack of concern, and so on.

The active listener is classically sitting reasonably upright leaning forward (into the conversation), jotting the occasional note and feeding back paraphrases to the person she is speaking to, and will often find herself making gestures such as nodding.

These gestures are not wasted; they are being translated through the tone of voice. Easygoing and friendly conversations may appropriately take place with the participants sitting back in reclining chairs with their feet on the desk, and this relaxation and friendliness produces an appropriate tone of voice too. Clearly the correct posture, tone of voice, and attitude depend on the conversation and the circumstances.

Bear in mind that it is difficult to fake the appropriate posture, tone of voice, and active listening, although it is very easy to fake the truth of the words being spoken. Therefore, from the listener's point of view, interpreting from the tone of voice to the posture often gives many clues to the genuine feelings of the respondent or meanings behind the words being spoken.

Mind Styles

It helps to understand something of yourself and the way in which you comprehend another person's manner on the telephone if you are to improve your own telephone comprehension.

Look at the ten shapes in Figure 6 very quickly and then, also quickly, complete them in any way that you think appropriate. Note that it is your immediate reaction that matters, so do not take time thinking through what you are doing. The shapes are such that you could produce letters very easily if you were of a mind to do so, or they could be the basis of pictures. The balance between letters and pictures that you have produced indicates something about the way your brain works.

All or mostly pictures

You are a visualizer. You tend to focus on pictures rather than the words. This usually means that you are very good at understanding the caller's emotional state and understanding the underlying meanings of what you are being told. Typically you may have trouble with detail and should make sure that you check as many facts as possible with the caller as you will tend to slide over them during the conversation. Visualizers tend toward creativity and rely on their intuition (appropriately so, because their intuition is well focused). They are not very logical people. Their general tendency, therefore, is to be working in the right brain (the artistic) rather than the left brain (the scientific). The visualizer's hobbies are usually of a creative nature. Visualizers tend to be diplomatic, perhaps sometimes to the point of being too euphemistic and not blunt enough for clear meaning when they are speaking.

Half letters and half pictures

Such people tend to be flexible, alert, and adaptable. They are generally the sort of people who are very good at running their own department or their own business.

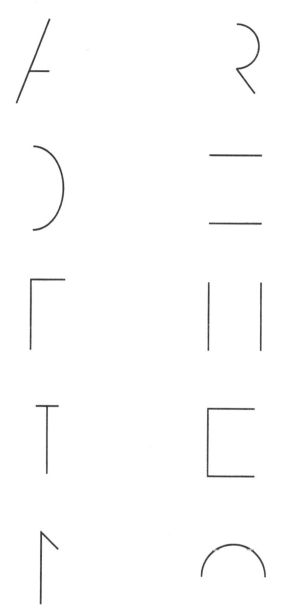

Figure 6 Complete these shapes as it "feels right" for you.

All or mostly letters

You are analytical. The analytical person is far less creative and will probably tend to have noncreative hobbies, such as collecting things. Analytical people like the telephone as a general rule and trust themselves to be good on it. Unfortunately, analytical people tend to believe the words they hear and might well miss the emotions and underlying meanings. They are easily manipulated on the telephone.

Covering for the Boss

Part of any secretary or executive assistant's job is to filter only appropriate calls through to her boss and deal with the others. This has to be done with diplomacy. At the same time, the secretary should not be asked to go beyond a certain boundary and must be able to retain her own integrity and honesty in work.

Be assertive, never aggressive or nonassertive

Throughout your telephone conversation (in any situation, in fact), you should always be assertive. Stand up for your rights while respecting the rights of others. If, for example, you have determined that the call is one that your boss would not want you to put through and that there is an appropriate alternative, the fact that the person calling is demanding to speak to your boss does not mean that you have to give in to that demand. Having stated that you cannot put the call through to the boss, and if through the conversation you continue to believe that is appropriate, then you should maintain that position with assertiveness. Aggressiveness or nonassertiveness allows other people to chisel at you and change your view of yourself and the situation, winning for them what they want while defeating you. The assertive secretary sets up win-win situations rather than win–lose situations. In this case all parties can win if:

- you do not put the call through to the boss, knowing that this is not what he or she would want; and
- you deal with the person's demands or inquiries in some other appropriate way.

Of course, the win for you is that you have done your job properly and effectively.

Do not lie

You have a right to your integrity, which must be established in your partnership with your boss. There are various tactful points following this that enable you to deal with the most common situations without lying.

It must be said that there are many secretaries who believe that part of their job is to lie for their boss. This book is not a moral tract, and any secretary that believes she should lie is of course entitled to act in that way if she feels it is appropriate (though we must state clearly that we do not believe it to be so). That said, it must or should be the secretary's decision and not a requirement of the job or effectively part of the job description. Certainly the degree to which a person should lie if she believes she must do so should be negotiated with the boss in partnership. (For example, a secretary might consider it appropriate to tell a caller that the boss is out when he is in fact in, but might not consider it appropriate to tell the boss's wife that the boss was working late last night when knowing that in fact she had booked him into a restaurant for two!)

Avoid asking who the caller is before you say the boss is in a meeting or out

There may be times when the boss is specifically attempting to avoid a particular caller she knows is likely to call that day. It may therefore be appropriate to find out who each caller is before indicating whether the boss is likely to take the call, but this should not be a general telephone behavior as it is very unsettling for almost all callers. If someone asks to be put through to your boss, then you ask who is calling and he gives his name, and only after that you tell him that the boss is not in, the caller is left with the feeling that had he been someone else the boss might well have been in.

It is worth finding a dialogue that is not a lie. If the boss is in, then it is a lie to say she is out, and if the boss is not in a meeting, then it is a lie to say that she is, but it might well be appropriate to say that the boss cannot be disturbed at the moment. Dialogues such as this are more honest.

The most appropriate course of action is full honesty. You should make it clear that all calls are dealt with by you or others and only put through to the boss on your responsibility and following a decision based on your understanding of the caller's needs.

This places on the caller the responsibility of explaining his requirements and gives you the fullest opportunity to find an appropriate course of action. If that, in your judgment, indicates that you should put the call through to the boss, then you should do so; otherwise you make it clear that you have to offer the caller another course of action. There will of course be certain people whom you know you will have to put directly through to the boss; in almost all circumstances those are the very people who will understand precisely why you are filtering the boss's calls. In many cases they will be aware of your relationship with the boss and will start the conversation simply by saying something like, "It's the managing director, please put me through to Mrs. Jones," knowing that it is appropriate for you to do so and indicating immediately your course of action.

Promise only what you can deliver

This means that you should not commit your boss to anything that he or she has not authorized or been aware of. For example, a person may say to you, "Get Mrs. Jones to call me back as soon as she is free." You should not reply that you will do so. It is not your place to make the boss's decisions for her, indicating whom she will call or when. Your reply should be, "I will make sure that she will get your message immediately and I will pass on the request you have made," or "I will ask her to do as you have requested."

Dealing with People from Abroad

English is the international language of business but it is not the English that most English people learn and speak. The international business language is known as

EFL (English as a foreign language). It is a limited form of English with standardized vocabulary and pronunciation. Politeness to foreigners using English as a foreign language demands a slower rate of delivery of speech and care to eliminate jargon and local expressions or slang. The expression "let's find a window in our diaries" is an example of jargon and is inappropriate for international use of English.

Caution with double meanings

The United States and the United Kingdom, it was said, are two countries divided by a common language. That division can become very apparent in business. For example, the expression "quite acceptable" in Britain would usually mean that a proposal was "averagely" acceptable; in other words, acceptable but not to any astonishing degree. In the United States, however, the same expression would mean very acceptable. "Quite" is a forceful word in America but a reserved one in England. Other expressions can be equally misleading. For example, in Britain, if we "table" a proposal it means that it should be put forward (on the table) and proceeded with. In America, however, "tabling" a proposal means that it should be ignored for the time being (what in Britain might be expressed as "shelving").

National characteristics

Effective communication is best achieved by being direct and speaking plainly. Psychologists have indicated that different nationalities have different ways of expressing themselves.

They have identified *high clarity* countries such as North America, Germany, and Scandinavia. People from high clarity countries speak very plainly, saying what they mean. For them the main purpose of communication is to transfer meaning. However, there have also been identified *low clarity* countries such as Japan and Middle Eastern countries. Rather than directly seeking to transfer information, people from low clarity countries enjoy the chase; in other words, language and communication is used playfully in getting to know each other.

When someone from a high clarity country tells you he believes your idea is of interest, then he probably means it. Someone from a low clarity country may be only trying to let you down politely, not feeling that it is worth pursuing at all.

The English, with their reputation for compromise, tend to fall between the two areas (no doubt becoming something of an enigma to those from other countries).

Humor and politeness

Humor does not travel well internationally. Jokes translated into foreign languages are rarely funny, particularly those that depend on a play on words rather than on visual images. Furthermore, people use humor for a variety of reasons other than making friendships: they use it to conceal their own uncertainties, to ingratiate themselves, to soften up opponents, and so on. Given that humor can become some-what ambiguous across international boundaries, people often suspect the worst when hearing it. Avoid humor unless you are absolutely certain that the person you are speaking to will understand it. This almost certainly means that you can only use it with people with whom you have already built a working and close relationship, probably face-to-face at some earlier time.

Country codes of politeness differ but obvious good manners will always be un-derstood and accepted. This is not a one-way street: people from abroad also take the trouble to learn our manners and will sometimes understand when something is a breach of their own national code, even though we find it acceptable. For exam-ple Americans and even some Britons get on first name terms very quickly but many Europeans insist on more formal titles (Mr. Jones, Mrs. Smith) even in long-estab-lished relationships.

Patience

Generally speaking, if foreigners are using your national language, you owe them a debt of patience to allow them to absorb in silence what you have said and to formulate their own reply. They will be concerned to deliver a reply to you that is considerate and polite but they may not have the skills to do this without some preplanning in their mind. Again there are national differences here. Anyone who has spoken over the telephone to a Japanese person, for example, will know that there are many gaps in conversation caused by this consideration, whereas any-one who has ever spoken to even a less than flamboyant Italian will recognize that any pause lasting longer than one second must be filled in by one party or the other!

Faxes

Use faxes as much as possible to send details, statistics, and long presentations to people from abroad so that they can absorb them in their own time. For complicated proposals, fax information ahead and then telephone at a later time. If possible, in-dicate on the fax when you will be telephoning in order that a person ready to re-ceive your call can be available, or at least the company you are calling can arrange for someone who speaks English to be available when you call.

Time zones

Remember that you will be dealing with international time zones. It will not do you or your business any good to telephone someone at 2 o'clock in the morning their time. If you work for a business with many international connections, then it is wise to have a chart of time zones available (showing adjustments for summer time or other countries' equivalents).

Resource bank

Put a circular out to all members of your staff and find out what foreign languages they speak. Have a list available, and make sure that the receptionist has such a list, so that if you receive a call from someone speaking a foreign language who cannot converse well in English, then you can call on that person to take the call and act as interpreter.

Dealing with Difficult and Persistent People

Inevitably there are times when you will be confronted by difficult, persistent, or even rude people on the telephone.

You have a right to demand reasonable language

No one can expect you to put up with abusive, derogatory, or threatening language and you have a right to warn the caller very quickly that if such language persists you will end the call. Any boss who fails to support that decision in reasonable circumstances will be failing in his responsibilities to you.

However, some people use bad language when they are in a panic. If you can determine that that is the case, then acknowledge that state and do what you can to reduce their panic. Almost inevitably they will then change their language behavior. For example, if you were to receive a phone call from an employee of your own company who was somewhere in the country trying to deliver a package by a deadline and could not locate the premises or person she had to deliver to (and who might rightly or wrongly believe her job was threatened by her failure) then you might have to extend extra tolerance and patience while assisting her. You can cool down emotions by asking for facts and offering solutions rather than involving yourself in the person's emotional state and offering her sympathy.

Some people use bad language when they are frustrated. Do remember that it may be someone in your company who is causing their frustration and you can do much to rebuild a good relationship if you can deal with that person's problems. For example, you may get a frustrated and abusive call from someone trying to make a complaint to your company and you may feel that it is unreasonable that he should be abusive when you are trying to help him. However, you may be the sixth person he has spoken to, with your five predecessors having forced the person to speak at great length about his problem before telling him that it was not them he should be speaking to and passing him on to someone they thought might be the right person. Again you might extend extra tolerance in those circumstances.

Never say, "It's not my problem"

When you are on the telephone, you are the company's store window. You are as visible to the person on the telephone as store windows are to a shopper walking down Fifth Avenue. You want your company to be as attractively presented as possible. If you are taking the telephone call, then it is your problem. You are on the front line and you must deal with the situation. If in fact you cannot solve that person's particular complaint or requirement, then it is your problem to find the person who can, rather than be dismissive.

Always be assertive

In telephone conversations, never be aggressive and never be nonassertive, as this leaves room for difficult or persistent people to cut in and force you into a position of doing something inappropriate, such as making an appointment that you know you do not want to make and you know your boss will not thank you for making.

Be repetitive when you know that you are telling the person what must be said (e.g., I cannot make an appointment for you but I can pass on a message to my boss that you want her to telephone you). The security that you are doing the right thing and that your boss will support you will enable you to be politely firm. (For details of assertive behavior, see Part 4, beginning on page 141.)

Dealing with Sales Reps and People Wanting Jobs

People will use devious means to get put through to certain people. For example, we made an arrangement with the head of training in a client company, virtually a "bet," that we could get put through to the chief executive despite the fact that all calls had to be circumvented by his secretary. We approached it as follows. First, we employed telephone sales techniques to discover what sports the chief executive was interested in. We telephoned, asking if he would be interested in a tennis promotion or football promotion and were told "no" each time. In the end (and perhaps as should be expected), we discovered that he would be interested in a golf promotion. We assumed that this indicated he was interested in golf. We then went to Companies House, where the home addresses of directors are listed, and got his home address. We then located the major golf courses near his home address. Armed with this information, we telephoned his secretary and told him that we were friends of his who regularly played with him at such and such golf course. We were put through to him directly without being questioned about our business. (He was rather unhappy about our circumventing his company rules until he was pacified by his own training manager, who pointed out the experiment that we had undertaken—and on this basis we were then asked to do some telephone training for his staff!)

The rules are very simple (applicable mostly to receptionists):

- Make sure you know your company guidelines covering whom you can put through to whom, whose secretaries deal with calls on their behalf, and so on.
- Have a list of people who can be put through to the chief executive or a particular director or manager; all other calls are to be put through to their secretaries.
- Only make offers that do not commit other people. For example, you can take someone's name and promise her that you will ask the person she is seeking to give her a call, but you cannot promise that she will be called. By passing the message on and asking the person to phone the caller, you will have complied with your promise, whereas you are not in a position to promise that she will be called.
- Never agree to anything just to be rid of a caller. You have to be the "stuck record." Having made your position clear, you must stand your ground.
- Never let implied consent go unchallenged. Implied consent is a technique of sales people. If they cannot get a direct invitation to come to your premises, they will say something like "I will be in your area next week and if it's all right with you I will drop in"; if you do not say, "No, do not do that," you have given implied consent and when they turn up they will say something like "I telephoned last week and made an appointment to come in today." Statements like "I will visit you," if met by silence, give the salesman implied consent to go ahead with what he has suggested. You must make it very clear if you do not want him to be there by saying, "No, do not until you are specifically invited to do so."

Dealing with People Who Do Not Know with Whom They Want to Speak

Many people will telephone, having only an idea of what they want and probably no idea of whom they want to speak to, which department, and so on. In order to deal with these people, you need to know your company like the proverbial back of your hand. Part of advanced telephone techniques is to make sure that you walk about the company and understand the physical structure of the buildings where the telephones are. In one case, in one of our client companies, there were many complaints that the warehouse telephones remained unanswered. Yet for some time, receptionists felt that they had done their duty by simply putting calls through; they did not report the fact that the calls were very often ignored, people were hanging up without being dealt with, and so on. It turned out that the warehouse telephones could hardly be heard in the warehouse and eventually louder bells had to be installed. Before that had happened, the receptionist should have been aware of the problem and able to warn the caller in advance that there might be difficulties and perhaps offer an alternative if the phone was not answered. Yet how many receptionists or secretaries visit all sites of say, a factory, in order to understand these problems? Be sure that you do!

To deal with people who do not know with whom they want to speak:

- Make sure that they have telephoned the correct company. It may be that your company name is similar to another's. Ask some broad questions about the nature of the inquiry to make sure that it relates to your product or your service.
- Make sure that you understand the nature of the inquiry. Do not make the person explain it in full and in detail or he will only have to do it again when you put him through to someone to deal with the inquiry, but be sure that you understand the broad nature of the inquiry so that you can put him through to the right person.
- Paraphrase your understanding of the inquiry so that you can be sure that you are both of the same mind. Offer him a name to speak to and tell him why you think that person is the correct person. Give him the opportunity of saying that it is not. For example, he might want to discuss a problem about a product and you might be offering him the complaints department when he wants technical services.
- When putting him through, announce to the person to whom you are putting him through that you believe she is the correct person but, if she is not, offer to take the call back so that you can deal with it. Do not leave the person you put the call through to find and transfer the call on to someone else. This is your responsibility. Do not force inexperienced phone users to do your job for you, calling around the company.
- If the caller is returned to the operator, then apologize for his problems and assure him that you—personally—will assist him until he is connected correctly.
- As always, remember to be in partnership with the caller.

Emergency Calls

The 911 emergency number is for the police, fire, and ambulance. Have available appropriate telephone numbers for the following emergency services:

- hospital;
- poison control;
- utilities (gas and electricity).

When calling the emergency services, have ready the following:

- The name and address of the person needing the service, which may not be you or may be a specific building in your company's office blocks.
- Directions for approach, particularly for large vehicles such as fire service vehicles, if there are complications or if the building is not easily found. Pay particular attention to making sure that you are aware of construction or roadblocks that might close certain sections of your premises and so on.
- A brief description of the problem.

It is important that you keep your descriptions to the emergency services factual and brief.

Look up in your local phone book the number dealing with gas emergency and have a prominent note of it displayed at your reception desk. Remember that anyone could report a gas leak from somewhere else in the building to you, expecting you to deal with that directly with the gas company. Also have the following numbers prominently displayed near the telephone and be sure that all staff know where these numbers are:

- the water company and a reliable contract plumber (for leaks, burst pipes);
- the electricity company;
- the nearest doctor.

Giving Very Bad News

The telephone is not the best way to give very bad news but there will be rare times when it is the only practical way to do so. Because giving bad news (death of a loved one, for example) is rare and rarely done by telephone, it is not the sort of area where you are likely to gain experience. Remember the following.

- Keep it brief but be ready to talk to the other party if she wants you to. Note that she probably will not want to talk to you, but will want to get you off the phone as soon as possible so that she can deal with her grief privately.
- Do not ask pointless tabloid reporter mentality questions like "How do you feel?" There is no sensible answer on offer and nothing you can do with the information if given it.
- Respond to requests for help or assistance as constructively as possible.
- Avoid using "I." You are supporting other people, not trying to compare their problems to your own. People who have just been given very bad news do not want to hear your very bad news and will gain no comfort from knowing that you have suffered as badly as they are currently suffering.
- Listen more than you talk.

Preparation for Making Outgoing Calls

There is a limit to the control you can exercise over incoming calls but you are able to make many more preparations for outgoing calls that you are making.

- Make the calls when you have planned time for them.
- Be in the right place for the call, preferably at your desk with a notepad, and not standing near someone else's desk or somewhere where you do not have access to files you may need.
- Know what you want out of the conversation. Are you making a complaint? If so, be sure in your own mind what remedy you want. Do you want a refund; do

you want a new item; do you want technical advice? Be sure that you are assertive in your demands.

- Make notes on what you are hearing. Remember the premise on which we started advanced telephone techniques: that you will remember 10 percent of what you hear, 40 percent of what you hear and see, and 70 percent of what you hear, see, and do. Making notes on what you are hearing forces you to see and do as well as hear.
- Close your eyes if it will help you to concentrate. (On the other hand, don't close your eyes when making notes!)

Ending a Conversation

Sometimes people make it very difficult to finish a conversation. There is a tried and tested three-stage plan that few people get past.

The first stage is: be honest, e.g., "I have to hang up now because I have a very tight schedule and I must go." This will weed out the vast majority of people, who sensibly take the point you have made and perhaps realize that they have been rambling inappropriately. It is polite because it makes the reason and responsibility for ending the conversation yours rather than any blame on their part but allows them a graceful way out.

For those who resist the first stage, try flattery, e.g., "I'll let you go now because I know you are a very busy person." You have politely pointed out to the most persistent of people that it is their fault that this conversation is going on too long and you are giving them a credible and flattering reason why the conversation should end. Even the most insensitive of people who get past the first stage usually bow out after this stage.

For the most persistent, put the ball in their court, e.g., "I have to go now because I have a meeting to go to but perhaps you could call me back so that we can discuss this further." What almost invariably happens is that the person realizes there is no reason to call back and nothing further to discuss and will then usually say so, e.g., something like, "Well, I think we probably discussed all we need to." In the unlikely event that someone does call you back, make it very clear that he had better have something new to say; if he is only going over the same old ground, then you should point out to him, "But we have already discussed this, haven't we?"

Saying "No"

Refusing an inappropriately made request is not always easy.

What not to do

Do not use an excuse such as "I would like to (do this, comply) but I have a meeting to go to." What will happen is that the person will latch on to the fact that you have accepted her request with a small deferment. She will then seek to arrange a time when you are able to do what she wants and you will have backed yourself into a corner because you have already agreed to.

Do not use a delay: "I will call you back and let you know." You are certainly entitled to ask for time to think about something if you genuinely need it for that purpose. It is a waste of time for you and the other person if you know already that you are going to refuse. Over time, it will get you a reputation for dishonesty.

What to do

Tell the truth: "I don't want to." Honesty will be respected. You might seek to temper the rejection with a truthful reason. You might also offer an alternative if you wish to do so. Be firm and polite, and remember to be assertive: you are standing up for your own rights while respecting the rights of others.

Getting a "Yes"

Many people seeking compliance to a request do not get it simply because they have expressed themselves badly or not made clear to the person they are speaking to what response they are looking for. (Remember the rules for saying "no" and remember that other people have the same rights as you.)

To improve your chances of getting a "yes":

- Know what you want and express it clearly. If you want a particular action or response from a person, ask for it directly so that there can be no ambiguity on the part of the person you are speaking to.
- Remember to KISS (Keep It Short and Simple). Do not swamp people with masses of facts or statistics. If such information is required, then fax ahead and telephone after they have had a chance to absorb the detail.
- Remember that the more arguments you put up, the greater the chance of losing one or more. It may seem that if you can put up 20 reasons for getting a "yes" instead of five, then you stand four times as much chance of getting a "yes." In fact the exact opposite is true. If you put up your five best arguments and they cannot be argued with, then you will be likely to get a "yes." If you put up 20

arguments and only one of them, being rather weak, gives the person opportunity for challenge, he will latch on to that one in order to deliver a "no."

- Be consistent and persistent. Be confident that you know what you want and stand your ground (remembering to acknowledge the rights of others).
- Find alternative ways to express the same thing. It may be that the person you are speaking to is not completely clear as to what you are asking or what you want from her and by expressing it in alternative ways you will give her a three-dimensional picture to work with.
- Look for common ground between the two of you and build on it. When you have agreement to some part of your request, build on that rather than on areas of disagreement.
- Know when to back off and try again. If you push the person to a definitive "no," then it is very difficult to go back and make the request again. If you feel that a "no" is coming, then back off from the request and try again later when you think the person might be in a more receptive mood ("He who fights and runs away . . .").

Preparation for Making Complaints

If you have to make a complaint, then you will lessen your chances of making a suitable impact or getting what you want if you "fire from the hip." There are some simple rules for effective complaining by telephone.

Give time for the emotions to cool down

If you get into your office and open a letter, which is the reason you are going to have to make a complaint, do not pick the telephone up while you are still reading the letter and begin shouting. Wait at least half an hour, which will give you time to absorb the letter. Consider wider ramifications and make sure that you are prepared for the conversation ahead. Moreover, know exactly who you want to speak to and be sure that you are not passed on to anyone else.

Have files and papers ready

When you make a complaint, you can be thrown if the person you call challenges your complaint and you are not in a position to defend yourself. For example, if you telephone the credit control company of a client asking them to pay your invoice and they say that they have paid it, you are left having to say something like "I will come back to you on this" if you are unable to respond immediately. What you should do is lay out the papers in front of you, read them, and be sure you are familiar with them. When you are told "But we have paid it," you can ask specifically for the check and date, check it against your records and point out something like, "No,

that payment was against such and such invoice, I am chasing this other invoice."
Be sure to review all papers before making the call.

Ignore excuses

Challenge excuses for what they are. Make notes on the papers that will enable you
to challenge excuses in the future. For example, if you are debt collecting and you
are told "Your check is in the mail," you may have to accept that as you cannot challenge it at this stage. However, if it turns out that your check was not in the mail and
it took you another couple of weeks to get a check from that company, then the next
time you phone them and they say, "Your check is in the mail," you can explain exactly what happened before and give a reason why you do not believe the excuse
being offered.

Silence Is Golden

In telephone techniques, we often concentrate on what should or should not be said
but it is important to know that there are times when *nothing* is to be said. By silence
you can create pauses that demand a response. All interrogators learn that when a
pause is created in the conversation, there is a great compulsion on the part of one
party to fill it by speaking. If you can learn to keep yourself silent, you have forced
other people to speak when perhaps they are trying to avoid doing so. For example,
if you say, "That is my last offer," then say nothing afterward; as soon as you break
the silence by speaking, you have diminished the impact of your "last offer."

Remember also to allow others a chance to think before they respond. Having
asked a question, it is not important for you not to keep filling up thinking time by
talking or your respondent will never have the opportunity to think through your
request and respond intelligently.

Getting Attention

To make a high-impact phone call, you should regard yourself as in a similar position to someone promoting a film. When they are advertising next week's film at the
movies, they put some very exciting film clips up on the screen to attract your attention. You should, in your telephone calls, also place priority on those things that
will be of most interest to the person you are speaking to (what's in it for him, what
advantage he gets by complying with your requests).

You should also use people's names appropriately so that people realize they are
speaking on a person-to-person basis rather than a company-to-company basis. Prevent people from hiding behind their corporations by putting their name into the
conversation occasionally.

Personalize, rather than depersonalize, your praise, and depersonalize your criticism. For example, if you wish to praise someone for organizing the office well, do not say, "The office is well organized," but say "You have organized the office well." On the other hand, if you wish to give criticism without giving offense, do not say, "You have made a lot of mistakes in the typing today," but rather say, "There have been a lot of mistakes in the typing today."

Additional Equipment

There are three aids to telephone communication that have special rules of their own.

Pagers

Many people carry pagers and you must know the company rules for dealing with these.

- Know when people can and cannot be paged (for example, are you able to page someone who is in a meeting?). If you receive a call and you tell the caller that you will page the person she is looking for, point out that there are certain situations where the person will not be able to respond to the page, in which case you will offer to take a message and ask that person to ring the caller.
- Make a clear note of the details of the call so that you are ready to respond to the person paged when he phones in. Have a note for the person that he should call or of actions that you believe he should be taking or considering.
- Make sure that when you leave your desk, for lunch breaks, messages for which you have sent out pages are handed over specifically to the person taking over so that she can respond to the person when he calls in answering the page you have issued.

Faxes

Facsimile transmission is a modern telephone technology and there are clear rules for both receiving and sending faxes.

Receiving a fax
- Check to see if an acknowledgment is requested and, if so, give that acknowledgment, pointing out that you will be taking that fax to the person for whom it is intended (you have then accepted responsibility for that task even if you delegate it to someone else).
- Make sure that the fax is sent to that person as soon as possible. (However, some people are beginning to use faxes to get a head start, in that letters go into an in-tray but faxes go immediately in front of the person concerned. Make sure that your company has considered when a fax genuinely requires urgent priority and when it should be regarded as just another letter received in the mail.)

- If the fax is incomplete or unclear as to meaning, then telephone and check the details. If a revised fax is required, make sure that that is sent before you take it to the recipient.
- Remember that a fax will fade quickly and if you want it to have a longer life, the fax should be photocopied.

Sending a fax

- Make sure that your fax machine has an intelligent station message on transmission. In a short hand of typing at the head of each page received by the person you send the fax to, there will be a station message, which is your company number and fax number. This is programmed into the fax. In one or two unfortunate circumstances, people have purchased or borrowed faxes from other companies, not changed the station message, and been for some time transmitting a signal that is an advertisement for another company and a number to which return faxes are often transmitted.
- Make sure that your fax header has a telephone and fax number prominently displayed for those who are required to respond. Make it very clear which number, extension, and name the person should respond to.
- Make sure that there is a contact name (perhaps your own) for those receiving the fax so that they can do as you should do when receiving a fax and acknowledge receipt.
- Give a clear indication on the fax of whom it is to be sent to in the receiving company.
- Remember that faxes can be used for special effects. For example, if your earlier correspondence has been ignored, a reply can be very effectively requested through a fax. It is like an open letter arriving in the office and can create some embarrassment among staff that might put added pressure on a company to respond to you.

Voice mail

- Consider the voice mail announcement message carefully to make sure that it meets callers' needs. For example, if you have a fax machine, you might also mention the fax machine number on the voice mail message.
- Always listen to messages as soon as possible, take written notes of the message, and make sure that they are distributed to anyone who should take action as a result of the calls received.
- Be sure to pass messages to people being called, using your message pad as if the call had been received "live," but noting on it that it was a voice mail message (see the message pad suggestions, page 61).
- Note the time the message was left, if applicable. Some voice mail features announce the time a call was received.

■ Where practical, phone callers back yourself and confirm that the messages have been received and passed on. Remember to tell the person that you have passed the message to that you have phoned the caller back and confirmed receiving that message.

A Set of "Rools"

The following are "guidelines for incompetence" that, we have found in our training, have become a humorous way to remember the basic messages of advanced telephone techniques.

The APW Training "guidelines for incompetence"

1. Always treat your caller as if he or she has just interrupted something more important that you were doing.
2. Be unfamiliar with and untrained on your equipment so that you stand a fair chance of cutting people off in the middle of a call or while transferring them. See if you can cut off at least ten people a day in this way.
3. Put callers through to extensions where there is no one to answer them, and never check to see if the call has been taken.
4. When callers from 3 (above) phone back to complain, put them through to the same extension.
5. Try not to know the names of anyone working in your company. Never learn their extension numbers.
6. Never know, or find out, the names of alternative people who could help callers.
7. Practice using these expressions: "I dunno" and "Huh?"
8. On answering, give the firm's name before you've raised the phone to your mouth, avoiding any chance for callers to know they got the right number.
9. When speaking, wedge the phone under your chin and be occupied with something else.
10. Let people finish giving you a complicated message. Then say "Just a minute, I'll get a pen."

My Personal Action Plan

You should complete a personal action plan as a result of reading this section. We have completed the first five points for you, and you should make sure that you complete the next five by the end of the week in which you have read this section.

1. I will create a message pad before the end of the week and get everyone in the company to use it.
2. I will always listen actively.

3. I will not distract myself when I am telephoning.
4. I will plan and prepare for my outgoing calls.
5. I will always see myself as in partnership with every caller.
6.
7.
8.
9.
10.

PART 3

Powerful and
Persuasive Writing

Because 90 percent of our communication is in speech, we need extra training and practice to make impact in the area of communication—writing—that we use so little. Secretaries are generally trained in typing skills and correct writing: layout and rules for letters and so on. The writing skill most needed in the present day is that of high-impact writing: knowing your message, getting it across effectively, and getting the desired result. Bosses need this support from their secretaries more than ever.

The objective of powerful and persuasive writing is to have the same effect on paper that you have when you are face-to-face with someone.

Where Is the Power in Communication?

Have you ever been told by someone that she hates you? Have you ever been threatened with violence? We hope not, but if you have, then you will have experienced, firsthand, a technique we use in corporate training to demonstrate where the power lies in communication.

Exercise 9

Find a willing friend to help you with this exercise. Tell that person that you hate him. Don't just say it; work yourself up to a state of real agitation and give a passionate blast from the heart. In training, we have seen people shout, scream, lean across tables, and even begin to cry with the anger they create. (Make sure you laugh and joke about it afterward!) Ask the person what impact you made. Invariably, he will describe your balled fists, your wide and staring eyes, the tension in your muscles, the way you leaned over near his face when shouting.

He will have become alarmed at the change in your voice—loud, harsh, and higher pitched—and will have barely noticed the words you spoke!

You can prove that for yourself.

Write down the words you have used and pass another willing friend a note saying exactly what you said to the first friend. She will not be at all alarmed or shocked. The point is that the first presentation had impact and the second did not. Yet the words were the same.

Repeat the exercise telling your friend that you love him. Use the same degree of passion. Be careful whom you choose here! (In our experience, around 50 percent of men go down on one knee for this, though I doubt they would in real life. Even nonverbals can be clichés.) Again, write down the same words and pass them to another friend. It will not have the same impact. Where is the eye contact, the touching of hands, the gentle and quiet tone of voice?

You can clearly see that the actual words spoken are not as important as the nonverbals: the tone of voice and body language. These nonverbals cannot be reproduced in writing, but there are alternatives. The proper sentence structure, choice of words, and—very importantly—use of punctuation can be combined to create writing that is not merely descriptive but also vivid. That is the essence of powerful writing.

What is most persuasive about writing?

People at work have a self-image of themselves as busy. Some genuinely are; many are because they manage time badly; even more make themselves busy (ineffectively) because they think they should be. A few more aren't busy and know it, but they don't want their bosses to know it. Therefore, everyone either is busy or acts as if she is. Your writing has high impact if it takes account of that self-image. Make it easy to read, easy to reread, and clear about what further action is needed. If it takes only a short time to scan through, then it will get read. A badly written document is not badly read, it is dropped into the in-tray for a later time, which may mean never. A badly written document is simply not read, or responded to, at all.

People are lazy

If you do their work for them by directing their attention to exactly what you want them to read, and tell them exactly how you want them to think, then the majority of people will go along with your proposals. Of course, your requests or recommendations must be sensible; no one is going to accept foolish suggestions. However, work situations usually come down to a choice of alternatives. If your alternative is well presented, it is likely to influence the reader.

People in business are looking out for themselves

When individuals read a proposal, or are asked to take a course of action, at least part of their brain is asking: "What's in it for me?" In your writing, put the "goodies" up front. Tell the reader what's in it for him, up high on the first page if possible. Take the trouble to seek out something to your reader's advantage and use it as a selling point for the report. We are not recommending overt bribes, but there are usually advantages to compliance that can be spelled out. They may be financial, but they are more likely to be career-oriented, or to increase the profile of the reader's department within the company. Whatever the advantages are, spell them out for the reader so that he is hooked from the start of your report.

Briefing

Briefing is not something that happens before the report writing job starts; it is part of the task.

Getting a good brief is your responsibility

An effective briefing will often indicate the form of the writing and, in some cases, will show that an alternative presentation may be more appropriate. Try to get briefs for large documents, such as reports, in writing. At the very least, make note of the main points of a verbal briefing and send them back to the person requesting the report for his confirmation.

The briefing must include:

- A clear outline of the problems, issues, or requirements that you are being asked to address.
- All deadlines. You do not want to spend three or four days working on a document only to be told, "Sorry, it was needed yesterday; it's no longer any use."
- Your limits of authority to demand access to information from other departments or individuals.
- Your resources: financial, workforce, use of equipment, and so on. Your research may even need a small budget if traveling and information gathering are involved.
- The reason for the document. What are you being asked to do, and why? To present facts so that others can form an opinion? To present an opinion? Or to present a counterargument?
- Reasonable access to the person requesting the document—usually your boss—so that when you have reached certain stages, or unexpected areas, you can communicate that fact and the report can be kept fully on course.
- The degree of confidentiality expected of you.

A lot of time can be wasted doing ineffective research, writing unnecessary reports, and wastefully spending time and money on projects that are not properly defined. Remember the golden rule: *the more effective the brief, the more effective the writing*. This applies to your preparation of it as well as others' use of it.

Get Ready to Motivate Others

To motivate others, your motivation should be recognizable to the reader. You, the writer, must share the vision for which the document is being prepared. The vision is something that starts with the person commissioning the document, though true motivation is not something that is handed down to others but rather is created by all those concerned.

The persons requesting the document should communicate the vision to you. If they do not share the vision with you, then your writing will be uninspiring. In the case of regular, or progress, reports, there must be a refocus of the vision every time a stage is written. Periodically there must be an examination of the need for, and the application of, the reports to determine if there are ways to make them more dynamic. There may be no way to dispense with reports, but they may at least be amended to create a more exciting use. Your beliefs in the quality of your work, together with a vision shared by you and your organization, are motivating factors for others.

Getting Yourself in the Right Frame of Mind

If you have difficulty in transferring your thoughts onto paper, the following tips may be useful:

- Talk through your ideas, preferably to a willing listener. Talking may help you to clarify your thinking before writing.
- Clear your head of emotional and other worries before writing. Try to organize a long, uninterrupted spell to begin with so that you can begin to "flow" in your writing.
- Where possible, do your writing in surroundings that are conducive to clear thinking.
- Promise yourself a reward for a job well done and—importantly—give yourself that reward when the time comes. It will make you feel all the better about the next document you have to write.

The above guidelines may not always be very practical in a working environment. For example, often you will have to work at your desk, although you think writing might be more pleasant elsewhere. Apply the suggestions with common sense.

The phases any writer goes through

Inexperienced writers are often shocked at the problems they encounter in putting words on paper. It helps, of course, to know that these stages are normal, but there are a few tips to make the process easier.

- At the outset, there is a daunting sense of the size of the task ahead. For a while, you will feel almost overwhelmed, and feel a sense of panic. Know that this is usual, and it will pass. What is happening is that your subconscious is beginning to get the task into perspective, and is beginning to plan an order of approach. Know that you are quite capable of doing the job, or you probably wouldn't have been asked. Set yourself a specific time or date when you will begin early stages of writing; then your mind will focus on the target date and plan your next stage accordingly.
- While your subconscious mind is "ticking over" the problem, it will randomly throw out ideas. Have a small notepad and pen with you at all times to jot them down. Keep them by the bed at night—the sleeping brain works on problems and offers solutions in the morning.
- Brainstorm ideas by talking them through with a willing listener, even if she has little to contribute. Tell this person your ideas and problems. Just describing them to someone else often clarifies them for you.
- Organize your data to make sure that you have covered the whole subject and that you have seen the necessary connections between topics.
- Write a rough draft without concern for style or impact. This stage will give you a foundation to work on to create the higher impact document. Imagine you are a sculptor with a large block of stone in front of you. What you are doing is chiseling out the basic shape before you put the detail in.
- Put the writing aside and forget it for a day or two. Come back to it with a fresh mind; it will be easier to see the strengths and faults in the writing. It will then be easier to carve out the finished product.
- Do not think of editing as a quick polish. Over half the total time spent on a writing project is in the editing. This is where the difference lies between something that does the job and something that announces its genius to the world.

You will see from the above list that you will need to budget for a lot of time that is not writing time: time to get in the right frame of mind, time to plan what to write, time between drafting and revising, and a lot of time for editing. Make plans for this from the start or you will run out of time and be forced to hand in an inadequate report.

Dealing with writer's block

Writer's block is the inability to turn your thoughts into writing, and occasionally the inability to think clearly enough to form an impression that can be transferred to words. Know that writer's block is normal, and happens to every writer at some time. Annoying though it is, there is a positive side to it. It is the equivalent of actors' nerves before going onstage—and any actor will tell you that when you don't have nerves is when you give a lackluster performance. Your mind is getting ready for the big moment. Nonetheless, the following tips will help you to clear the block and focus on the writing task at hand.

Clarify the desired outcome of the writing. Is the report to make a recommendation? To counter someone else's recommendation? To explain something to an expert? To explain something to someone who knows little about the subject? Just by clarifying this point, and perhaps talking it through with a willing listener, you will refocus your attention on the overall task, and clear a block that might have formed by your losing a sense of direction.

Rather like a speech stammer, writer's block can worsen as you recognize that it is happening. The treatment is the same as for some stammering: find a "key" that will release it. In the case of a stammer, it is a word that you find easy to say; in the case of writer's block have a game you can play. Try writing one paragraph of your report as if to a child, or to the president, or to whomever you wish. This new angle can make writing a fun game, and you will begin to flow again.

Don't be surprised to find that some concepts are hard to grasp. Some concepts *are* hard to grasp. It isn't writer's block. Writing contains some real hard work—and we're sorry, but there's no cure for that!

Writer's block can come from worrying about how the final product will be received. Remember that in most cases the audience is on your side—they want you to be successful. Your boss wants solutions, and a well-written document may well promote one. He will be looking positively at it, provided you have achieved a proper standard of research and effort.

Organizing Your Thinking

You cannot write until you have an overall view of the whole project. Use visual mind-mapping aids, as described below, to help you to create that big picture.

Mind-mapping

The example in Figure 7 is based on a company's decision as to whether to provide cafeteria facilities. By organizing your thinking along the lines shown in the figure, you can identify gaps in information, in work undertaken, or in conclusions drawn. You can then fill in the missing information or adjust your ideas accordingly.

This form of mind-mapping is very useful for gathering together the results of brainstorming exercises or lots of seemingly unrelated information that you have to arrange in logical fashion. At the center of Figure 7 is the principal point of issue: in this case, the decision that our premises will have a cafeteria. From this, we can see that there are five main areas requiring study:

- the need for a cafeteria;
- the site of the cafeteria;
- the decision whether or not to contract the work out;
- the food that will be supplied;
- other uses to which the cafeteria might be put.

Each of these main areas can then become a subsection that other people can collect data for, reporting back to you. Alternatively, you can tackle one area after another without wasting time going over the same ground or missing obvious stages.

Having isolated both the main issue and the principal aspects to be dealt with, you can isolate particular areas of work for consideration. Occasionally, there will be connections between the main areas and these will reflect crucial points that need particular research or more detailed study.

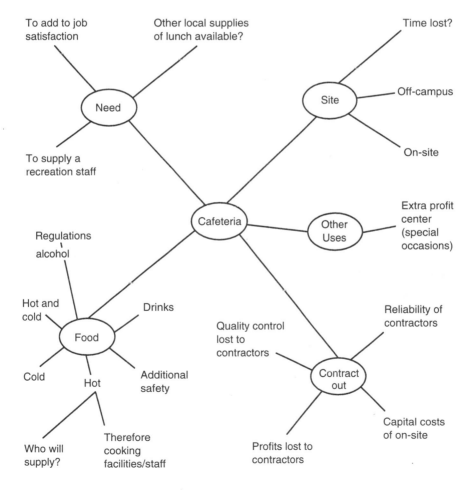

Figure 7 A typical spider diagram.

Start by putting the main issue in the middle of the page. Then draw off the main points. Gradually filter down the scale, drawing off points from each issue, and points from the points. The whole project can be mapped in this way. In large projects, you will need submaps. The main map may have a central, main, issue and several points drawn from it, the submaps may start with one of these secondary points in the center and draw more detailed points off, and so on.

Your document should include the right number of facts

How many facts do you need? You might well argue that the more facts you can present the more effective the report. This is not so. If someone asks you for a book, he will have less trouble finding it in a pile of three than if you point him to a floor-to-ceiling bookshelf.

Your job as a writer is one of synthesis. The reader needs only the pertinent facts set out in a logical order; so eliminate any irrelevant ones. To do this, first list all the facts that you think might be relevant. Then ask of each, "Why is this likely to be useful?" If you cannot come up with an answer, or you cannot think what use your reader will make of it, then leave it out of the document.

Bear in mind your deadlines

In the real world, you may not be able to produce a perfect, finished product (though you should aim to do so). There may come a time for a trade-off between a full set of facts and meeting your deadlines. Management information—the basis of most business writing—must be presented in time to be of use.

Where to Start

Perhaps surprisingly, you must start your writing by concentrating on the end.

Start with the reader in mind

Imagine your writing in the hands of, and under the eyes of, its readers. Then ask yourself:

- Are the readers interested?
- Do they understand what I have presented to them?
- Will they act on my suggestions?
- Are they moved and motivated by my writing?

Only then can you work backward, visualizing how the document must look, getting the right data at the right time in order to organize it, to create the writing you visualized them reading.

Many people write from their own perspective: "If I have something to say, information to give, or suggestions to make, then provided I 'have my say,' the job is done." Consider that argument in the context of a personal presentation: If you have had your say, did it do any good if you were talking in an empty room? It is up to anyone making a personal presentation to make it one that the audience wants to see and hear. Imagine a production of *Hamlet* where the actors thought their own performance was not going to make any difference, and the audience were there only because they needed to be, not because they wanted to be. It would be pretty dull stuff! Similarly, as a writer, it is up to you to make the reader want to read your writing. And bear in mind that *need* is not the same as *want*. The person who needs to read your writing may be a captive audience, but he or she may not act upon it. Whether she feels motivated (wants) to do so will depend in part on whether you have addressed what she wants as well as what she needs. The only realistic starting place for good writing is to consider the reader. So ask yourself:

- Who is my reader?
- What is the impact I want to have?

Dealing with several readers

The reader may or may not be known to you. Although individual knowledge of the reader can help when drafting a piece of writing, it is not crucial. Indeed, you should always maintain your business relationship with the reader, and not a personal one.

Often, however, there is more than one reader and this may affect the impact of your writing. To have a desired impact, you should address the reader on her own terms. But, clearly, it is not practical to write specifically tailored documents for each intended reader. One piece of writing must suffice for many, and therefore you must address the common interests of the group. For example, if you are preparing a report to be read by a board of directors consisting of 20 people, then in thinking reader first you should consider the common requirements of the board. The writing should create the same impact upon all of them, if properly addressed, though this is something of an oversimplification. In some respects, the sales director will, of course, have different requirements from the production director.

If the report is to be read by not only the entire board, but also line management, workforce, and contractors, then clearly one report will not do. Variations must be prepared—each addressing the requirements of a specific group of readers—because it is fair to assume that such diverse groups will have diverse requirements. The same report cannot create the same effect in widely different groups of people.

A reasonable compromise may be to send the same report to the various groups, but with different, and specific, covering memos that direct each reader to their areas of interest, or the areas that you want them to be interested in.

Communications

When you try to express your emotions, opinions, and feelings about a project to another person, you have to translate these abstracts into words. There is always something lost in that translation, and in the translation back to abstracts by the recipient. This is the basic problem of all communications.

Communication models

The translations are being blocked by a series of "filters." Your experiences will color your viewpoint of the subject being written about. These experiences—from potty training onward—will have created your values, opinions, attitudes, and beliefs, and those ideas you regard as facts.

After you have sifted your message through all the above filters, you have to translate it into code (language). The language will contain suggestive meanings often quite unintentionally included, but relating to your experiences. There is an abstract level in all writing that reflects these values, opinions, attitudes, and beliefs. You may not notice this unless you take time to consider it. Examples of communications follow below.

The problem is made more complicated when you recognize that all that is stated above about you, the writer, also applies to your readers. They also have values, opinions, attitudes, and beliefs. If it is difficult for you to prepare a clear and unambiguous message through the barriers of your own filters, it is even more difficult to navigate through your readers' filters. Figure 8 shows a communication model.

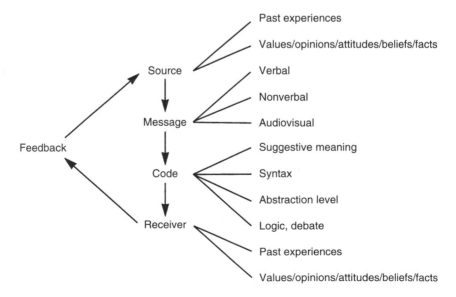

Figure 8 The communication model.

Let's look at examples of flawed communication. Only by seeing how communication can break down unintentionally can you be ready to avoid the pitfalls.

"Jacklin holed out at one under par, but Nicklaus took a bogey."

Is this an effective communication? It is only effective if you and the reader share common experiences, knowledge, and background, at least to a sufficient degree. The expressions *holed out*, *under par* and *a bogey* are definitive and unambiguous but are jargon words from golf. Two people with an interest in golf will understand the expressions; those with no such interest may find the expressions meaningless. Jacklin and Nicklaus are famous names in golf and may be known to you and your reader. To people who are not well versed in the subject, the names may mean little or nothing.

"Jacklin beat Nicklaus decisively."

This is even less effective. The word *decisively* is not definitive and will mean different things to different people, even two golfers. One may believe decisively means "by more than two strokes (points)," whereas another may think it means "more than four strokes." Other players will have other interpretations. In business writing such matters cannot be taken for granted. Clarity can only come from precision. The sentences would give the full names of the players and the exact score, without value judgment as to what constitutes *decisive*.

"Brahms holed out at one under par, but Liszt took a bogey."

Communication breaks down here because Brahms and Liszt are not associated with golf. If there are two players with those names, then more detail about them will be needed to make clear to the reader whom you are referring to. The names Brahms and Liszt are associated with music (and drinking!), where common knowledge shared between you and the reader would not encompass the references to golf.

"My provitt has become more disturbed."

This cannot be communication. The word provitt has been made up for this book and cannot mean anything to anyone because there cannot be a common ground of knowledge. Any impression of a message in this sentence is purely the creation of the mind of the reader.

The world picture

For effective communication, you have to create a world that the reader can understand. It is very easy to leave out important details because your mind is filling them in as you write. The danger is not that your readers will be left with a blank, but rather that your readers will assume certain images from their minds. These images may be quite different from those in your mind. This might create a wrong impression.

Consider the following sentences.

"John was assigned to his company's office in England. He went to live in

London, and bought a vehicle. He courted a young lady named Penelope but she came to prefer a friend of his."

This seems to be a good communication. Quite probably you—as the reader of this book—have an image in your mind of the situation. But how similar is your image to the image held by us, the book's authors?

"John went to live in London."

We might all have a picture in our mind of John in London, but what picture? The West End, with John amid the lights of Piccadilly Circus and the loud noise of frantic traffic? Or is John in a quiet, leafy suburb? Is John in London in 1995? Or 1895? Or 1595?

Even if we decide on Piccadilly Circus in 1995, we must be careful not to convey hidden images. Piccadilly Circus in 1995 might be glorious lights, exciting theaters, and ebullient street life to some, but might be a world of beggars and drug addicts, danger, and despair to others. Both views probably have truth; neither is wholly true. So we need a clear description of when John went to London, which London it was, and what part of it he went to.

"John bought a vehicle."

Even if we agree that John is in the capital city of England, in Piccadilly Circus, in 1995, there are still a wide variety of vehicles available for our mental image. Some of us might imagine an automobile, others a van, others still a motor bike. If we narrow this down to an automobile, then what car? A Ford? A Lamborghini?

Without more facts, our impression will be created by several factors. We might have an image of the sort of man John is, wealthy or not. We might have taken a liking or a dislike to him. Based on that, we might assign to him the car we would like, or one we would wish on our worst enemy. So for a picture, we can both understand we need an unambiguous description of the vehicle.

"He courted a young lady named Penelope."

The expressions used here will mean different things to different age groups. *Courted* may mean something quite genteel and *olde worlde* to some, but quite modern to others. The expression *young lady* may similarly have certain hidden messages for different people.

There are many hidden subliminals in our writing; we found another in the above example. Over the years we have used this example, we have monitored certain impressions created by the writing. Over 80 percent of men under 40 believed that Penelope had blonde hair; when pressed most admitted that the only Penelope they knew was the puppet on a TV program they had seen, Lady Penelope, and she was blonde. The key was triggered by our accidentally linking the two words *Lady* and *Penelope.*

"She came to prefer a friend of his."

When? It could be that John and Penelope married and lived together as husband and wife for 30 years, and then she eventually preferred a friend of his. Alternatively, she might have come to feel that way after a matter of days. Whenever she *came to prefer a friend of his*, what was the result of that? Did she leave John to live with the friend? Did she stay locked in a loveless marriage, pining for the other friend? Was the friend male or female?

For your message to be clear, it is necessary to build a picture of a world that is unambiguous. We now have a definition of unambiguous: something that is not dependent on the abstract understandings of individuals.

Get commitment by expressing your commitment

- Put enthusiasm into your writing. Don't be afraid to gush. There is nothing wrong, and everything right, with using expressions such as "exciting possibility" instead of "satisfactory result."
- If your document relates to an ongoing project, then make sure that success and accomplishments already achieved are adequately recognized and praised.
- Your writing should exhibit confidence in the readers and should believe in their success. Those expected to achieve will do so more frequently than those who are expected to fail.

Use influencing techniques

You will seek to influence or persuade the reader toward your own viewpoint. Such influencing skills should be honest rather than manipulative; the reader should be attracted to the demands of the writing rather than pushed into its conclusions. Examine the driving forces that will encourage people to accept the conclusions of your writing and the restraining forces that will prevent them. The document should prominently state the aspects that will encourage the reader.

To encourage the reader to accept the recommendations of a piece of writing, you should point out the advantages of compliance and say why you believe it represents the best possibilities. You should not expect your writing to succeed on the basis of "if you don't comply then you'll be fired." Such an attitude may well get compliance in the short term but it will be because of forcing your reader reluctantly into action, rather than a more enlightened persuasive style, taking your reader along with you. Negative techniques that are poor in motivation and short-lived are usually based on fear. In the corporate environment, fear is usually the threat of redundancy, change of job status, and so on. People may be forced to act but in the long term will seek some form of revenge for the humiliation they suffer. The more enlightened your reader feels then the more long term and genuinely committed to your view he will be. Achieve this by sharing a created vision with the reader; encourage him to take responsibility for his work based on your writing. Persuasive styles take longer to get results, but the results are longer lasting.

Build new ideas on old knowledge

New and radical ideas do not suddenly arise. Even inspiration is usually the product of a process of logical deduction by the person so inspired. However, what seems logical to you may be so radical as to be virtually illogical to anyone else. Because of this gulf between your mind and the mind of your reader, it is important to understand that you cannot present a new idea or new knowledge without building it on a foundation of old and accepted knowledge with which the reader is familiar.

There is psychology behind this difficulty that relies in part on attitudes toward change. New ideas, new concepts, new knowledge, and new procedures all represent changes to the way people do things or perceive things. Generally speaking, people are excited by change. However, when it is presented to them in an inappropriate way, there is an initial resistance caused by the fear of the unknown. New ideas presented without a foundation of old knowledge therefore appear to be the unknown and are automatically resisted. If you build your new idea on old knowledge, much of the resistance is mitigated because the change does not seem so radical or so frightening.

An example of this is where departments are the subject of a program of computerization. If a department receives a report that simply states that, as of Monday, the department will be changing over from a manual system to a computerized system and explains only the details of the computerized system, then there is an obvious danger of panic by people within the department who cannot see how the changeover will be made without severe disruption. If the steps that will take people to the new computerized system from the existing system with which they are familiar are explained, the panic is reduced or removed.

Be sure to anchor your proposals on something your reader is familiar, and comfortable, with.

Make clear connections between facts, arguments, conclusions, and recommendations

Make sure that the conclusions you arrive at, and the recommendations you make, are supported in the text and not just in your mind. If you follow all the advice given so far to plan and draft your report, there should be few leaps of logic and your report should be clear to its readers.

Never be vague, always specific

The more specific you can be, the more persuasive your writing will be. If you state that there will be "significant savings" if your proposals are accepted, your reader can do no analysis of this. If you state that your recommendation will "save $5000 per annum for the next three years," there is a clear quantity that can be analyzed by the reader, and put into context by him in assessing the merits of your proposal.

Vague terms meet resistance from readers who believe that the vagueness hides something to be wary of (and it often does!). Precision gives confidence to the reader.

Be positive, be optimistic, and offer solutions rather than problems

Use positive, optimistic language. If there is a negative to be expressed, find the positive way to express it, thereby offering a solution rather than a problem. Instead of "We cannot begin phase two until we have your signature of approval" (something we cannot do), use "As soon as we have your signature of approval, we will begin phase two" (something we will do).

Part of being positive is to use positive words. For example, use the word *questions*, which implies the existence of an answer, instead of the word *doubts*, which suggests only uncertainty. Add to this principle the offering of solutions instead of problems. Replace "If this raises any doubts in your mind, please let me know" with a more positive version: "If this raises any questions in your mind, please call me and I will answer them."

Use of jargon

Jargon is not outlawed but must be viewed with caution. Jargon is the technical vocabulary of specialists, such as chemists, accountants, lawyers, mathematicians, legal secretaries, and so on. It is quite proper for them to have their own jargon, which enables them to communicate concepts within their own field of expertise in a simple way. The important point is one of communication. Expressions such as *highly geared* will mean something to accountants; therefore, a report from one accountant to another could comfortably use the phrase without loss of clarity. Using jargon in this way is a way of saying, "I am in the same club as you." However, for a specialist to use specialist jargon to outsiders is inappropriate. The expression *highly geared* may not mean anything to a nonaccountant and it is therefore not an effective communication. Far from saying "I am in the same club as you," it creates the implied suggestion "I am in a special club that you are not in"; an attitude guaranteed to annoy any reader. Bear in mind, then, that jargon used in writing that will be, or may be, read by outsiders can become pompous and irritating, and is best avoided.

There is a further caution. As a nonspecialist do not use jargon to specialists, even if it is their jargon, unless you know that you are at least an honorary member of "the club." It creates the impression of trying to ingratiate yourself. In Tom Wolfe's book *The Right Stuff*, test pilots described how they became extremely irritated by newsmen and others using their jargon phrases such as *augered in* (meaning *crashed*), which amounted to an invasion of their private world by outsiders. The other danger of using other people's jargon is that it is often more subtle than it seems and it is easy to use it mistakenly, making your case seem all the weaker.

Make your report a
Raiders of the Lost Ark film script!

Well not really, but hold this image. It is a technique in such adventure movies to have planned exciting bits to keep the audience's attention and to move the film along. Naturally they have to be spread out. When you're writing your report, find interesting bits to keep the reader's interest. Spread them out throughout the report. Imagine a film with all the action in the first ten minutes and then two hours of Indiana Jones reading a book in his garden. How many people would watch Jones read a book for two hours even if they knew there was an exciting ten minutes at the end?

When you sit down to write a report, *hold the image* of the film as a model. Several trainees from our courses have said, months and even years after our courses, that they still make it a ritual to spend five minutes planning the action in their reports before drafting.

Persuasive words

Consider the following 12 words:

money	easy	health
you	love	proven
save	discovery	guarantee
new	results	free

These are held to be the 12 most persuasive words in selling to a wide audience. They are employed extensively in junk mail, often highlighted to emphasize their importance. These words will change over time; no doubt environmental words will join the list if that subject is thought to have become of interest across age, sex, and social boundaries.

We don't suggest that you try to employ these words in your business writing. However, it is worth taking time to find words that would be appropriate and highly persuasive for your readership. At least a few of these words should be employed in the opening, selling paragraphs.

Exercise 10
Find 12 persuasive words that will influence your boss or staff to make a change in your department that you think is significant.

Punchy Writing Style

Business writing is never a work of literature. You are not going to get the Pulitzer prize for your efforts, and writing that looks as if you might be trying for it will feel uncomfortable. Consider the following outline tips in constructing the writing.

Paragraph structure

A paragraph is a group of sentences with a common theme. The sentences within it relate to the same topic and should describe and develop it logically. The correct length for a paragraph is: long enough! Paragraphs today are shorter than they were 100 years ago, a reflection of the present-day demand for short, quick, concise groupings that can be assimilated quickly. Keep paragraphs logical and clear; aim to keep them to the shortest sensible, practical level.

Sentence structure

In business writing, effective sentences are short and sharp. Complex sentences are difficult to understand and tedious to read, particularly if the reader is pressed for time and seeking to extract information easily. Vary sentence lengths, but keep them short. We recommend an average sentence length of approximately 10 to 20 words. There must be variation in sentence length to prevent the report from becoming monotonous.

Use of end weight in sentences

Because a sentence ends with a period, which creates a pause, the last few words in the sentence will be strongly imprinted in the reader's memory. Therefore, the key phrase in the sentence should come at the end.

For example, if you want to describe the circumstances of a fatal car crash and you regard the crash and the fact that it caused death as the most important aspects of the sentence, then you would make less impact with "the fatal crash was caused by another car" and greater impact with "another car caused the fatal crash." (If you regarded the significance of the other car as the most important point, then the first sentence would have the greater impact.)

The rule is to get all the facts into the sentence in such a way as to shock the reader into an appreciation of the importance of what you are trying to express.

Use the beat of triadic text

Consider the wide application of the number three in our everyday lives, where logic would not suggest that this number was of any significant importance: three-piece suits, three-room suites, three-bedroom houses, and so on. This rhythm of three is strong in our communication patterns: Julius Caesar came, saw, and conquered; Hollywood's earliest heroes were all tall, dark, and handsome.

If a sentence must convey more than one simple idea, then consider the power of a triadic arrangement of text. Complex sentences with a beat of three are often used by newspapers: "When the miners were released by the rescuers, all were exhausted, some were in a state of shock, and a few showed terrible signs of physical injury." In this sentence, there are three basic references to the condition of the miners. This is powerful reading, and creates memorable images. To extend beyond three references, however, would weaken the impact of the sentence.

Use active, not passive, verbs

A verb is *active* if the subject of the sentence is performing an action; the verb is *passive* if the subject is receiving an action. An example is "Mary was admired by me." Because Mary is the subject in this sentence and is receiving the admiration from me, the verb is passive. In the sentence "I admired Mary," I am the subject and performing an action—admiring Mary—so the verb is "active" and has higher impact.

Adopt a perspective to write from, and to write to

Write either to a person (you) or from yourself or your company (I or we). Be consistent. For example, the following memo to warehouse staff, shows inconsistency: "Warehouse staff must examine deliveries for shortages. If you locate items missing report these to the supervisor." The writing shifts from the *third person* (the warehouse staff) to the *second person* (you). To correct the inconsistency, the memo should read: "Warehouse staff must examine deliveries for shortages. If staff locate items missing, they should report this to the supervisor," or "You must examine deliveries for shortages. If you locate items missing, report these to the supervisor."

Keep vocabulary up-to-date (but not faddish)

Business writing can sound out-of-date because writers use an inappropriate style of language, often borrowed from the legal profession. For example:

Avoid	*Use*
We are in receipt of your report . . . (be specific)	We received your letter/communication . . .
Please arrange to return . . .	Please return . . .
It has come to my attention . . .	I noticed . . .

Keep your use of language
up-to-date, and write as you would speak

This advice is not intended to encourage the use of slang. (One of the authors was working on a container base in London and was invited for *muggo*; the docker's expression for afternoon tea. Outside that group, this would not be widely understood.)

Be wary of new words and
phrases entering the language

Coined phrases or idioms often go out of style quickly, or are not universally understood. You must judge such phrases as they arise, but the rule is not to force them into your report in order to look up-to-date. If they seem to be appropriate, then they may well be. (But pause for thought when editing.) Examples of such phrases are:

This is doable.
We need a ballpark estimate.
I'll find a window in my diary for the meeting.
Can you give me the bottom line on these figures?

Do not use phrases, particularly new ones, if there is any reasonable likelihood that they can be misunderstood.

Keeping to a neutral gender

Gender deserves a mention of its own because of social changes in recent years. Women now comprise a huge section of the business world at all levels of authority. It is important to reflect a neutral gender when writing to a wide, and often unspecified, audience.

Avoid such phrases as "The manager should consider his staff requirements" (implying masculine managers only). Replace such phrases with "The manager should consider his or her staff requirements" (reflecting both masculine and feminine) or "Managers should consider their staff requirements" (moving to a neutral, plural, pronoun) or "Managers must consider staff requirements" (eliminating the pronoun altogether).

Be thoughtful and creative in keeping to a neutral gender. Too much overuse of *his* and *her* or *s/he* makes writing hard to read (in this book we use *he* and *she* alternately, and their use doesn't reflect any value judgment). As a general rule, use plurals: they avoid references to gender but retain a personal quality. However, be sure not to use *they* or *them* to refer to one person (e.g., "When someone phones you, ask them for their telephone number").

How to Use Punctuation

For persuasive writing, punctuation should be seen as a tool of reading rather than writing. Use punctuation to make the reader's task of understanding your material easier. For example, proper use of commas, semicolons, colons, and periods will allow you to breathe for the reader. If there are long passages of text unbroken by punctuation, then readers find themselves holding their breath as they read, waiting to be instructed when to pause (the same sort of effect as holding your breath when watching long sequences of underwater filming). Similarly, the eyes need to blink to replace the coating of moisture that lubricates them. Pauses allow for programmed blinking, making the reading more comfortable.

Use punctuation to make your writing more comfortably readable, making sure never to lose the ABC of business writing: accuracy, brevity, and clarity. Within these guidelines, bear in mind the explanations and rules of punctuation that follow.

Comma

A comma is used within a sentence to show that the flow of the sentence is being interrupted. The comma marks the shortest of pauses in a sentence. It can replace the word *and* in sentences, moving the flow of the text along faster. For example, better than "The man picked up his handkerchief and his pen and his keys and his watch," is "The man picked up his handkerchief, his pen, his keys, and his watch."

The comma separates independent clauses in a sentence to increase the clarity of otherwise complex expressions. "The pen may be mightier than the sword, but it is still easier to write with."

The comma separates a phrase in any part of the sentence. For example, "The company, which always purchased expensive properties, made a substantial profit." This allows for two related points to be made in one sentence. The clause in this instance is called *nonrestrictive* because the sentence could stand without it (i.e., the company made a substantial profit). If the clause was an essential part of the sentence—that is, the sentence would not be effective or meaningful without the clause—then the commas would be omitted. For example, "The man who is happy is the man to employ." In this case, the clause is "who is happy," and it is essential (restrictive) because without it the meaning would be either unclear or wrong. Here the directive is to employ not just men, but men who are happy.

When using commas, remember that their placing will affect not only the reader's pauses, but also comprehension. Consider the phrase "Caesar entered on his head, his helmet in his hand, his sword in his heart, a love of Rome overwhelmed him." It reads correctly as "Caesar entered, on his head his helmet, in his hand his sword, in his heart a love of Rome overwhelmed him."

Semicolon

A semicolon represents a longer pause than a comma but shorter than a period. It is often used to link clauses. For example, "Truth ennobles man; learning adorns him."

Where clauses already contain commas, then semicolons can be used to encourage the correct pace and pauses in the reading of the sentence. "He was with Charles Smith, the governor; Jane Brown, the mayor; and Mary Green, the senator." In this case it is clear that he was with three people. Those three people were Charles Smith, who was the governor, Jane Brown, who was the mayor, and Mary Green, who was the senator. Without the semicolons, it would be unclear if he was with up to six people, or what job titles they held: "He was with Charles Smith, the governor, Jane Brown, the mayor, and Mary Green, the senator."

Colon

Another device for inserting a pause into a sentence, the colon produces a longer pause than the semicolon. A colon is used to precede lists and summaries. For example, "The doctor noted various symptoms: high blood pressure, migraine, and nausea." The colon is also used to introduce long, and usually formal, quotations. For example, Roosevelt said: "There can be no fifty-fifty Americanism in this country. There is room for only one hundred percent Americanism."

There is one further use for the colon that might appear in a report, though its use is usually restricted to literary style. The colon can be used as a tool of emphasis to stress a final word or clause. For example, "I put his success down to one factor: stubbornness."

Period

The period marks the end of a sentence. Overuse of this end punctuation can make writing childish and tedious. For example, "The file is red. It is thick. It is in the top drawer of the cabinet." This is more effective if written as "The file is red, thick, and in the top drawer of the cabinet."

Question mark

A question mark is used at the end of a question. For example: "Are you able to help with this?"

The question mark is sometimes used, though less commonly nowadays, in the middle of a sentence containing a series of questions. For example, "Does Howard like Jane? or John? or indeed anyone?" Because convention has steered the question mark to the end of sentences, it is generally better not to use this form but to reserve the question mark for the end of the sentence only. This avoids confusion on the reader's part. The sentence would be written: "Does Howard like Jane, or John, or indeed anyone?"

Questions can often be subtle commands. For example, "We should do this, shouldn't we?" This might well be a command, particularly if delivered by your boss. However, in business writing, the use of a question would be taken literally and would be seen to seek a response. In business writing, if a command is intended, then it should be clearly given.

Exclamation mark

Exclamation mark are usually inappropriate in business writing. They are used to replace the verbal tones and body language of shock or surprise, neither of which ought to be in a business report. In literary style they might be used to emphasize, as in this sentence: "The rat actually put it in writing!" This is not factual enough for business style. If the actions are the cause of complaint, then make the complaint intelligently. As a tool of emphasis, exclamation marks might occasionally be used, but very rarely and with caution.

Apostrophe

The apostrophe denotes the position of a missing letter in certain words. For example, *don't* instead of *do not*. It is appropriate to use these in business writing, particularly where it helps to keep the style from becoming too formal.

An apostrophe also denotes a possessive. For example, the cat's tail. Where the possessive relates to a plural, the positioning of the apostrophe changes, appearing after rather than before the *s*. For example, the cats' tails.

Writers seem to have a particular problem with its and it's.

- *It's* is a contraction of it is; it is not possessive. The apostrophe denotes the missing letter.
- *Its* is the possessive. There are no apostrophes—as there are none in other possessive pronouns, such as hers and his.

Parentheses and dashes

Parentheses and dashes are used to enclose an intrusion into a sentence. Examples are "The experiment described (see page 12) has been successful," and "The directors announced—as the Union suspected—that the pay rise was going to be lower than that of last year."

Distinction between the two can be subtle. In spoken delivery, it is possible to use tone, pitch, and volume of voice together with body language to emphasize or detract. In writing, parentheses are often used to detract, in other words to enclose items of lesser importance, whereas dashes often enclose emphasized items.

Quotation marks

Quotation marks, or inverted commas, can be either double ("") or single (''); in both cases they are always used in pairs. One of the pair opens the quotation or title, and the other closes it.

Quotation marks denote direct speech. For example: "I hope you are feeling well." Quotation marks are also used to denote titles of articles, poems, and conferences. Single quotation marks are used for titles within titles or quotes within quotes, such as in dialogue.

Capital letters

The first word of a sentence always starts with a capital letter. Certain words always start with a capital letter, even if they arise in the middle of a sentence. These are: proper names (Simon, London); days of the week and months of the year (Tuesday, June); the first words of directly quoted speech (She said, "He was feeling ill"); names of organizations (World Health Organization, United Nations); titles of books, magazines, and so on (*A Tale of Two Cities*).

Hyphen

The hyphen is a device used to combine words. Its use is regarded as transitional because combinations of words eventually become acceptable in their own right. For example, *folk lore* became *folk-lore* for a time, but in later dictionaries became *folk-lore*. Sometimes the hyphen is used to join an adjective to a noun, e.g., the red-eyed office manager.

Use of abbreviations and acronyms

There are so many rules offered regarding abbreviations, often themselves not consistent, that we offer here a simplification to make life a bit easier. You will find other recommendations in other books; you must choose the style you feel comfortable with.

Many abbreviations are shortened versions of longer words. In these cases, a period is used to indicate the shortened word, e.g., Jan. (January) and other months. But shortened words that have now become accepted as words in their own right should not carry a period. These words are now included in the dictionary, and used without being meant as abbreviations. Examples are: bus (omnibus); flu (influenza); fridge (refrigerator); plane (airplane); and zoo (zoological garden).

The overriding rule is that the abbreviation must be clear to the reader. Even if it is in common use with you and your immediate peers, consider that the reader may not understand the abbreviation; worse, in certain circumstances there may be confusion arising from overlapping possibilities. For example, the acronym—the shortened version of a group or organization—CIS could stand for the Cooperative Insurance Society, could now also stand for the replacement to the Soviet Union, the Commonwealth of Independent States.

If there is likely to be any doubt, spell out the full name. One way of making the abbreviation clear to your reader is to write out the full word(s) when first used, with the abbreviation in parentheses; then use the abbreviation thereafter.

Homophones and homonyms

There are many words that sound either identical or similar but that have quite different meanings. Often the wrong word is used in a report, causing some confusion. The main difficulty with computerized spell-checkers is that homophones and homonyms will be accepted by the computer as they are valid words. Examples include:

their	there
possessive: "their room")	(geographical: "it is over there")
weather	whether
(rain, wind, and snow)	(whether or not)

Clichés

Clichés are phrases that have become worn-out and ineffective through overuse. They sound superficial, have a low impact, and fail to carry strength in their meaning. They have been described as the "fast food" of language. Examples of clichés are "at the end of the day," and "in the ball park."

Clichés give themselves away by sounding hollow and stale as you read them. Whenever you find such an expression in your writing, search for a new way of saying the same thing, bearing in mind that the new way should still be clear, concise, and of high impact.

Figures of Speech

Generally speaking, figures of speech add color, emphasis, and vibrancy to language. They are very useful in spoken language, and effective in written literature. However, in business writing they should at best be used with great caution, and usually not at all, because of the ambiguity they can cause.

Antithesis

An antithesis consists of contrasts illustrated by the arrangement of words. An example is "To err is human; to forgive, divine." This is not usually appropriate for business writing.

Colloquialism

A colloquialism is an expression in everyday use, and should be avoided in reports except in exceptional circumstances, where it prevents overformality. Examples are "the room was a mess" and "I offered to give him a hand." The main disadvantage of colloquialisms is that they are vague and will have different meanings for different people. For example, what constitutes "a mess" to one person may be tidiness to another. It is this ambiguity, rather than the informality, that is not appropriate for good business writing.

Epigrams

Epigrams are short, witty, satirical statements typical of writers such as Oscar Wilde. For example, "in married life three is company and two is none." Epigrams have no place in business writing.

Euphemisms

Euphemisms are mild and deflating expressions used to replace a blunt and realistic one. For example, "pass away" is often used as a gentle replacement for "died." In business writing, a factual description is more important than a tactful one. In business, dead is dead!

Hyperbole

A hyperbole is exaggeration used for the sake of emphasis. An example is "he died of laughter." Such an expression does not belong in business writing. To people from other cultures, such expressions are confusing.

Malapropism

A malapropism is the deliberate misuse of polysyllabic words, substituting a wrong word for the correct one for the sake of humor. The two words must be very similar in sound and style. An example is "she was as headstrong as an allegory on the banks of the Nile" (allegory/alligator). This is definitely not to be used in business writing. Sentences so constructed are deliberately meaningless at face value, and it would be impossible to predict the interpretation many readers would make.

Metaphor

A metaphor is a part of everyday speech, a use of a phrase that includes a description by comparison, therefore suggesting a similarity. For example, "the curtain of night came down" compares the onset of the darkness of night with a lowered curtain.

Clearly it is not factual, but it creates an image that describes the event and, perhaps, the writer's feelings about it. Almost certainly this should not be used in business writing.

Onomatopoeia

Onomatopoeia is the use of words that suggest their meaning by the sound they make in pronunciation. Examples are crash, slap, and bang. There may be occasions when the inclusion of a word to describe a sound is appropriate in business writing: for example, "There was a loud 'pop' when the chemicals were mixed." If you use one, put the onomatopoeic word in quotation marks to show why it is being used.

Paradox

A paradox is an apparently self-contradictory statement that is nonetheless true. For example, it was said of one famous pop star that "his appearance was carefully untidy." This is a contradiction in that untidiness is usually the result of lack of care rather than carefulness. However, the whole statement may be true in that the pop star did look untidy but in fact wished to look so, and took a great deal of care making sure that his appearance was untidy. This is not appropriate for business writing because the contradiction makes the meaning uncertain. In this example, take the time and extra words to describe his appearance, and state why you believe it was deliberately contrived.

Simile

A simile is a literary device where one idea or object is likened to another in order to emphasize a particular aspect of the one. Examples are "dry as a bone" and "quick as lightning." Because they rely on the shared world of reader and writer, and because they often become clichés, similes should be avoided. If you are certain that you and your reader will share the meaning correctly, they might be acceptable.

Other Points of Grammar

Split infinitive

A split infinitive occurs when, typically, the word *to* (the sign of the infinitive) is separated from the infinitive (the verb). An example is "He did not want to entirely surrender his position." In this example, *to surrender* is the infinitive and the word *entirely* is splitting it. Here it is unnecessary and the sentence would read better as "He did not want to surrender his position entirely."

There are occasions when splitting an infinitive gives greater clarity and the rule here must be that to split an infinitive is acceptable if it adds to clarity or to ease of reading. Avoidance of split infinitives, once demanded of good writers, is now subject to circumstance. Indeed, in some cases a completely mistaken meaning can arise from an effort to keep the infinitive intact. Consider the following examples. If you want to express a situation where someone has openly asked someone else to be discreet when dropping a hint:

1. He was asked to discreetly drop a hint.
2. He was asked to drop a hint discreetly.
3. He was asked discreetly to drop a hint.

In the first example, the infinitive is split but it is easily understandable and reads well. It is clear from this sentence that the manner in which he should drop the hint should be discreet. In the second sentence, it is unclear precisely what *discreetly* is being used for. It may relate to the way the hint should be dropped, or the way the request was made. The third phrase, like the second, keeps the infinitive intact but actually says the wrong thing; in this case it seems that the person asking him to drop the hint did so in a discreet manner and that he is free to drop the hint in any way he wants. As you can see, the first phrase is the clearest although it does split an infinitive.

Ending sentences with prepositions

It has become permissible to end a sentence with a preposition if that makes the sentence clearer and easier to read. In this example *in* is the preposition of the sentence: "In which room is the meeting?" is less comfortable to say and read then "Which room is the meeting in?" The latter is therefore preferred.

Use of contractions

Using contractions such as *don't* for *do not* or *won't* for *will not* is acceptable providing that the style does not become too loose and chatty. A reasonable use of contractions makes business writing less formal, and more friendly to read. There may be occasions when writing is expected to be very formal in style, in which case contractions will be inappropriate.

When to use "I" and "me"

There is often confusion over when to use *I* and when to use *me* in certain sentences. For example, should it be "Charles and me will be pleased to look at your proposals," or "Charles and I will be pleased to look at your proposals?" In this case it is "Charles and I."

The test is simple: remove the reference to the other person and see how it would then read. You would not say "Me will be pleased . . ." You would say "I will be pleased . . ."

In this next example the same test applies: "Telephone Charles or I for further information" or "Telephone Charles or me for further information?" Remove the reference to Charles. You would say "Telephone me . . .," not "Telephone I . . ." The second sentence is therefore correct.

Using "and"

And is overused in writing, creating a childish style that is difficult to read. The proper use of *and* is to join two short sentences of roughly equal complexity and importance. An example is "Mike is the Finance Director, and Sarah is the Sales Director." For more complex relationships between sentences, such as where the second sentence arises as a consequence of the first, *and* should not be used: "This report is important, and it must be sent to the Managing Director." The sentence should be reconstructed to show the *cause and effect* relationship. "Because this report is important, it must be sent to the Managing Director."

And can also be replaced by commas where it is linking lists in sentences.

Latin and foreign phrases

Latin and foreign phrases should be avoided in business writing because it is not always clear what they mean. They are often used by writers to show an intellectual superiority over their readers, which is precisely the wrong type of relationship to build with your readers.

There is no foreign or Latin phrase that cannot be expressed just as well in plain English, and this presentation will be appreciated by the reader. Many foreign and Latin phrases are not listed in standard dictionaries, which may make it difficult for the reader to translate, causing considerable irritation.

Typical phrases include:

ad valorem:	according to value
bona fide:	genuine
caveat emptor:	let the buyer beware
inter alia:	among other things
ipso facto:	by the fact itself
per diem:	daily
noblesse oblige:	privilege entails responsibility

One secretary was reported in the national press as having misheard her boss's dictation of *ipso facto* and sending out a letter, to a portly individual, containing the phrase "if so, fatso."

It would be unreasonable to rule out certain phrases that are in such popular use that they are very well known. Examples of these are:

curriculum vitae (usually reduced to CV)   an account of one's life (Latin)

(This is used in job applications and job advertisements. We would not recommend its use being widened beyond that particular application.)

graffiti	scribbling (Italian)
postmortem:	after death (Latin)
pro rata:	in proportion (Latin)
status quo:	things as they were (Latin)
vice versa:	the other way around (Latin)

All these might be acceptable but exercise discretion in their use, and avoid overuse.

Ambiguity with dates

Many reports are read internationally but the conventions for dates are not internationally agreed upon. For example, in the United States, a date is written as month/day/year; in Britain, it is traditionally written as day/month/year. Therefore, 7/8/92 would be interpreted in Britain as 7 August 1992 and in the United States as July 8, 1992.

When you are writing dates in a report, do not refer to the month by a number but rather by its name, which may be abbreviated (Dec. for December, for example): December 21, 1992, for example.

Overqualification of words

Business writers often overqualify words for emphasis. In many cases, these overqualifications add nothing to the meaning of the sentence and in extreme cases detract from it. Examples follow.

Incorrect	*Correct*
completely useless	useless

(If it has no use at all, then it is useless. Any further qualification cannot make it more so.)

in actual fact	in fact

(There are no nonactual facts.)

very true	true

Overqualification usually arises when you try to emphasize a point you feel strongly about. Examine the areas of the writing you are most committed to and check that in your attempt to stress points you have not made these mistakes.

Example 2

One enlightened writer's account of desynonymization distinguishes between negative desynonymization, such as this example, and positive, morally progressive desynonymization, such as the words obligation and compulsion, a moral sophism upon which the philosophy had been based, and which had been exposed by several philosophic writers of the late seventeenth century. The writer's own attempt to desynonymize this literary undertaking is the modern equivalent of this assault on skepticism and materialism, and an important aim of the analysis. But the sundering of property and propriety, the failure of legitimation on the part of the propertied ruling class, demands the intervention of a moral or intellectual aristocracy to set things to rights and substitute a new principle of social authority.

There are 115 words in three sentences, giving an average of approximately 38 words per sentence. There are 35 polysyllabic words (words with many syllables): enlightened, desynonymization, distinguishes, negative, desynonymization, example, positive, progressive, desynonymization, obligation, compulsion, sophism, philosophy, several, philosophic, seventeenth, century, desynonymize, literary, undertaking, equivalent, skepticism, materialism, important, analysis, property, propriety, legitimation, propertied, intervention, intellectual, aristocracy, substitute, principle, authority. A total of 35 polysyllabic words in 115 is approximately 30 percent, so the fog index is $(38 + 30) \times 0.4 = 27$.

This is virtually gibberish and quite beyond the capacity for easy reading of anyone with a normal vocabulary.

Bear in mind from the above examples that neither is actually outlawed or inappropriate in its own context. The first example is most appropriate for a child's early reading lessons; the second example may be appropriate within a certain peer group.

Neither is appropriate for business writing. The appropriate readability index for business writing is about 12. This reflects an easy-to-read usage of adult vocabulary. Use the fog index to test your work occasionally and see how readable your work is. Aim to be heading toward this figure of 12.

To summarize how the fog index works:

1. Select a piece of writing of approximately 100 to 120 words and count the exact number of words.
2. Count the number of sentences and calculate the average number of words per sentence.
3. Count the number of words of three or more syllables. Exclude words beginning with a capital letter (proper names) and compound words that are of three syllables or more because they are made up of two words, such as bookkeeper or stepfather. Do not count words that have three syllables only because of the addition of endings such as -es or -ed, e.g., created, advises.
4. Calculate the percentage of words of three syllables or more (polysyllabic words).

5. Add the average number of words per sentence to the percentage of words of three syllables or more.
6. Multiply the total by 0.4. (The figure of 0.4 was calculated as a conversion rate based on the number of years of formal education a reader of average intelligence would need to read and understand a particular piece of writing.)

One word of caution: do not write a piece of work especially to test your fog index or you will tend to cheat, designing the outcome that you want to achieve. Take a piece of work that you have done in the past week or so and use that.

Adjusting your writing for your readership

There are many reasons for adjusting your style of writing.

First, your own style of writing may not be readable to your own peer group. If you are to be easily understood, then your writing must be aimed toward the readers within that peer group. This is not usually a problem as most individuals in a group develop thinking and talking in the same language.

A second reason for adjusting your writing is that other readers, particularly those outside your peer group, may have a language style different from your own. By leaning toward the style of writing that would be appreciated by your reader, your report will be that much more user-friendly.

Third, there is the question of appropriateness concerning the material being presented. The clearest example of this is in journalism, where the same piece of news may have to be written in different styles to be appreciated by the different readers of different newspapers. An article written in the language style of *The New York Times* probably would be regarded as pompous to readers of *The Daily News* and it is quite probable that an article written in the language style of *The Daily News* would not be appreciated by *New York Times* readers.

Exercise 11

Write a headline and a paragraph for different publications. Take a film that you have seen recently and write a headline and opening paragraph reviewing the film for the following publications:

- *The New York Times*
- *The Village Voice*
- *People Magazine*
- *The Wall Street Journal*
- *Electronic Media*

Exercise 12

Write a welcoming note for a new employee just joining your company or department. Use the following different approaches:

- genuinely welcoming (warm and friendly)
- sarcastic
- hostile
- cold and aloof
- making sure they know you're the boss
- overfriendly

Extending your vocabulary

All writers should seek to extend the range of their writing vocabulary. People have four ranges of vocabulary:

- Spoken vocabulary. This contains the least number of words (on average 4,000 to 12,000 words). It is the language used in conversation.
- Writing vocabulary. When writing, people use a wider range of words than in speech.
- Reading vocabulary. This includes words not used in speech or when writing, but which are easily recognized when reading.
- Recognition vocabulary. This is the widest range of our comprehension of words, often containing over 50,000 words. Apart from words spoken, written, or recognized in reading, it includes words not generally recognized but that may be recognizable when seen in a context that is familiar. By way of example, you might use the word *mate* in conversation but would use *friend* when writing. You might never refer to a friend as *an intimate* but would understand it if you read it. Alternatively the expression *an intimate* might not be meaningful to you, but you might understand the meaning if it arose in a context that indicated friendship.

How to extend your vocabulary

The way to extend your vocabulary is to read. Have a dictionary on hand to look up unfamiliar words. Use them in your writing when they seem comfortable and appropriate. Don't force the use of words beyond what is comfortable or your writing will become formal and unfriendly. Furthermore, using words without a clear understanding of context can result in using the wrong words in a certain situation.

Warning: Reading a dictionary will not extend your vocabulary because dictionaries offer no experience of context. The best first step in extending vocabulary for many people is to read a higher level newspaper. The sensationalist tabloids use simplistic language. If you are writing business reports, you will certainly need a vocabulary range more extensive than offered by these newspapers. Don't go straight to the business newspapers; there is a very suitable range between the two.

Editing and Revision

Having written a rough draft, you must spend a great deal of time and effort in editing. This is where the writing is really crafted from the rough outlines. If time permits, allow a week or so to pass before going back to the writing. This will mean that your preoccupation with certain aspects of the writing will have passed and the report will be refreshingly new to you. You will be able to inject new ideas and new life into it. If time does not allow, then you probably did not plan very well for all of the preparation stages. The main thing is not to edit right after writing, giving yourself no opportunity to come to it with a fresh mind.

Do not pass your writing over for final typing without revision on the basis that "It's probably not as bad as it seems." Most people adopt this approach only when they can't face just how bad it is and, far from being "not as bad as it seems," it will probably be worse. Be honest with yourself. If you feel that major revision is needed, do not throw the draft in the wastepaper basket and start again. If you do that, then there is a very real danger that you will follow the same logic and end up with the same writing days, weeks, or months in the future. Whatever you have done had reason; start from that point and build to the final document.

Go through the draft checking that the style, layout, and contents are consistent. Check that the reasons for the document lead to the work done, which—in turn—leads logically to the findings and the conclusions, then the recommendations.

Writing and editing are different

Remember that you cannot do a proper job of writing and editing at the same time. Writing is creative; it is exciting and experimental. You should allow ideas to flow, though at this stage they may be poorly developed and badly situated within the draft. Editing is a critical process, challenging your own thinking. Editing ensures that ideas are properly developed, and placed in the right context. You cannot be creative and critical at the same time.

Editing takes time

Attributed to many people, most famously Winston Churchill, is the quotation: "I am sorry I had to write you a long letter as I did not have time to write you a short one." This reflects the truth that editing takes time and effort. The first draft is long and rambling; the edited final product should be brief, clear, and to the point.

Take care to connect logical facts

The edit stage is the time to make sure that, although your writing may be factual, accidental connections have not been made. For example, you might want to compliment your department on its end-of-month computer shutdown. You might also want to point out in the report that your boss was away at that time. Both statements are factual. However, if you write "The computer shutdown was very well managed. The boss was away at the time," you might be implying that the shutdown was successful because the boss was away. This would then create an unfair, or inaccurate, impression.

One test for these accidental connections is the use of a "Napoleon's idiot." There is a story that when Napoleon wanted to make sure that all his generals would understand an order, he would first give it to one particular general who was notably stupid. If that general could understand it, anyone could. This led to the phrase "Napoleon's idiot" for someone who could test a report for clarity. The term is not meant to be derogatory. The expression means using someone not as familiar or expert in your field; she may well be an expert in her own field. This person should not be someone involved in the report. Give this person a draft of your document to read and ask her to let you have her general comments as to layout, format, and clarity of explanation. Remember, you need to know how clear it will be to anyone who reads it.

Circulate drafts of your writing for comment

Circulate drafts of your writing to key interested parties for their comments. This has two main advantages. First, you will have feedback from people who are end users of the writing as to its readability, suitability, and so on. Their comments will enable you to incorporate changes into the final document that will be of benefit to all readers and, ultimately, to you.

Second, this method of involving others in the final document means that they will feel committed to the writing. They will already be receptive to its findings. They will feel that they have contributed, and their commitment will therefore be all the greater.

Guess the political effect of your document

Before final circulation, consider the political implications of the document—the reactions that it will generate within the company, particularly by those strongly committed to, or opposed to, the material and your conclusions. Anticipate possible reactions and distribute the document with tact. Consider these points when constructing your follow-up.

Disclose information
informally where possible and useful

There may be people who cannot have access to your writing but will be affected by it. Where possible—and without breaching company regulations or confidentiality—discuss the main features of the material with them.

Information Technology

Business writing can be greatly enhanced with the application of modern technology: word processors, spell-checkers, computerized thesauri, electronic mail memos, graphics, and all-in-one software. This section is a practical guide to these techniques and when to use them, outlining ways to use them most effectively. With laptop and notebook computers, considerable storage space and easy and quick access facilities are available in highly portable form. Combine this with the range of software programs available, such as style-checking programs (examined below) and it is perfectly feasible for you (should you be so inclined) to sit in the middle of a field with a small portable notepad computer on your lap and type a highly complex business report in a fairly short time. While sitting there, you can have a software program check through the report for more than 20,000 common mistakes of grammar, punctuation, and style.

Much of the drudgery of writing will be replaced by developments in computerization. You should keep up-to-date with available hardware and software. This should not become an excuse for allowing standardization and machine programs to replace your flair and intuition; rather it should remove obstacles from your work to enable you to concentrate fully on creating the very flair and drive that good writing should have.

Word processing

Your most obvious computerized aid to a report writer is a good word processing program. The word processing program is to the typewriter what the typewriter was to the quill pen. Common as they are, these programs are still far from being in universal use and it is worth giving a brief description here of word processing. You input content through a keyboard not dissimilar to a typewriter keyboard, but containing a wider range of capabilities. Instead of appearing on paper coming out of the typewriter the typed words appear on a television-like screen or *monitor*. The document typed is then stored on a disk where it can be retained indefinitely. Copies of the document are printed off on paper as needed. There, any close similarity between typewriting and word processing ends. Having got a first-draft document on the screen, you can manipulate that document before committing it to a hard copy (i.e., paper printout). Most word processing programs offer the following facilities.

- There is a range of type styles so that when printed the document can combine several different typefaces as well as italics, boldface words, underscored words, and so on.
- Sections of the draft can be isolated and moved to other parts of the writing using a simple electronic cut-and-paste facility.
- Sections of the writing can be copied to other sections so that the original remains where it is but a copy is transferred to another area of the document, or even another document, very quickly.
- There is a range of other useful abilities available to make the writing more attractive or quicker to edit, e.g., justified margins that make the print end in a straight line on both sides of the page, just like the page you are now reading.

Besides the above, many word processing programs allow you to set up templates (standard outlines) so that certain documents can be prepared on a pro forma basis. If, for example, you have to prepare a monthly report of figures in a certain format, the outline where the figures are inserted can be kept as a template on the computer. Rather than having to be retyped each month, it is called up and you insert the figures. Because of all these features, it is possible to modify documents for particular readerships. Templates also prevent you from having to reinvent the wheel. If you begin a new job, then you will have the standards set by your predecessor available for your immediate use.

It is possible to give documents to others for editing or comment by sending a copy of the computerized document on a disk. With networked systems, many workstations can access the same disks; then even the physical transfer of a disk is unnecessary. A person at another screen, possibly in another room or even on another continent, can call up your work and make his or her own comments on it, and it is instantly available for you to examine.

The ease with which drafting and redrafting can be done allows for experimentation in a way much less available with handwritten or typewriter text. It is perfectly feasible to allow someone to call up a template and play with it, just to see what they come up with. The time and resource cost is much lower than it would be if the person was uselessly experimenting with handwritten drafts that were then being passed to secretaries, edited, passed back, redrafted, and reprinted. This allows for radical thinking and the easy development of new ideas. The word processor's adjustibility allows you to type as you think. It has freed many writers from dependency upon a secretary or access to a secretarial typing pool. The increasing low cost of this technology has encouraged many people in the business world to have their own word processing capabilities outside the office.

Most programs have a built-in spell-checker with a fairly extensive dictionary, allowing an easy check of the spelling of the most commonly used words. These dictionaries also enable you to insert words of your own choosing. Besides spell-checkers, many programs have a computerized thesaurus that offers a range of alternative words. Beware of overtrusting your computer. Overdependency on computers is dangerous. There is still a tendency for people to believe a computer when it says that everything is all right, but it should always be remembered that the computer has its limitations.

There is a humorous story of someone putting the phrase "The spirit is willing, but the flesh is weak" into a computerized translation program to convert it to Russian. The Russian translation was then fed back from Russian to English. Far from coming back in its original form, it came back as "The meat is rotten, but the vodka is strong."

Spell-checking

It is very easy to believe that if a document has been fully spell-checked by a computer, then all the spelling in the document must be correct. This is not so, principally because there can be many spellings of similar words all with different meanings. We have seen one piece of writing that contained the (spell-checked) phrase "flexing his mussels."

Thesaurus

Far from being an aid to clear writing, a computerized thesaurus can often be a hindrance, encouraging you to search for more complex words than necessary. Use this aid with caution.

Computerized writing analysis

Probably the most radical software available to business writers using word processors is the range of grammar-and style-checking programs available on the market. One such program analyzes writing, searching through and offering advice on 20,000 common mistakes. One analysis performed is a statistical summary of the following.

- Total words in the report.
- Average sentence length. Generally, the longer the sentence the more difficult it is to read.
- The sentence length distribution on a bar graph.
- The number of passive verbs in use in the report, which translates into a passive index. This is a measure that you can attempt to manipulate in order to increase the impact of the report.
- A summary of common mistakes, including: complex words, jargon or abstract words, overused words, legal words, clichés, business clichés, redundancies, overwriting, foreign words, passive verbs, hidden verbs, misused words, confused words, hyphens, misspellings, British spellings, grammar errors, sexist words, and foreign words.

Some of these programs allow for a personal style to be inserted into the program.

Most style-checkers allow for editing to be done directly on the word processor screen, or print out the advice so that editing can be done by hand on paper for those who prefer that method. Some style-checkers have a different flexibility in that they are not only geared toward report writing. One such program allows for a selection from a series of writing styles: business, technical, fiction, and informal.

Distribution of Your Documents

There are basic rules to follow when you have completed your writing and it is ready for distribution.

- Be sure that your distribution list is complete and up-to-date. Make sure that people are in the departments you expect them to be in, and that their titles and positions are correctly noted.
- Consider whether there are other people who ought to see the writing or who will be offended if they do not. Make sure that they get a copy or that you are able to discuss the material with them.
- If the documents are being mailed, make sure that specific instructions are given as to whether the mailing should be first or second class, registered, and so on.
- If possible, deliver documents by hand (particularly within the same building).

Follow-up

Even if your writing is persuasive, powerful, and clear, and creates the right impression in the mind of the reader, it might not get acted upon. The problem is that business documents often have a low priority. Many people work on the basis of doing what they are pushed to do and assume that everything else must be unimportant. Your job is not finished when you have completed the writing; the document must get acted upon and it is your job to make sure that it does.

Some documents do not need follow-up. A report of an event that happened, which is recorded for archive purposes, needs no more follow-up than to ensure that it is properly filed in the archives. However, for many documents there is a subsequent action expected. There are several actions you can take to make sure that your writing is being used.

- Make personal or telephone contact with people who you expect will be involved in the implementation of your ideas and discuss issues with them. Make it as formal or informal as you consider appropriate but make it clear that you have the material's impact on your mind and that you will be pursuing its progress. If people can feel your enthusiasm for your recommendations, that enthusiasm will be contagious.
- Where there is a clear next step, spell out exactly what people should do now. Get their commitment and see that they do it. If there are easy and quick stages,

make sure that you follow up with a telephone call or personal meeting to ask whether that stage has now been completed. Ask for a one-paragraph memorandum or summary of the results of that action (or more if required).

■   Consider making a presentation of the main recommendations of the report before distribution.

■   Your document may take some time to implement and there may be several stages or several different implementations. Issue updates showing the progress of other people's actions arising from your writing.

■   If your document is to appear on committee or department agendas, obtain copies of those agendas and make sure that it does. If it does not, then arrange a meeting with the chairperson or secretary of those meetings to find out why it has not been included.

Duties of the Reader

The efforts of both writers and readers can change a company's whole writing culture for the better. As a reader, you have the opportunity, and the duty, to help create good business writing. Do not accept a badly written document or, worse still, spend your time correcting someone else's mistakes without his knowledge. If you receive poorly written documents and do not comment on them, then you deserve to continue receiving the same because the signal you are giving to the writer is that what he is doing is acceptable. If it is not acceptable, make this clear.

As a reader, if you accept effective and well-presented writing without comment, then the effect is to demotivate the writer. Where praise is due give it, preferably openly and in person, with enthusiastic body language and praising verbal speech.

How to Write Large Documents, Such as Reports

Having set out the ground rules for writing generally, and taken account of the problems of communication, we must begin to focus on the writing task itself.

Only start drafting when you have the overall purpose

If you simply start at the beginning, there will be a tendency to ramble because you will convince yourself of your own arguments as you go along. There will be a lack of commitment, or overcommitment to certain points, and the writing will be jumbled because it will reflect jumbled thinking.

Consider the process of writing a popular mystery. It may be only on the last page or two that the writer reveals whodunit, but from the outset of writing the book he or she will have already determined the identity of the villain. If the writer did not decide until the last line who the villain was, the book would hardly be a taut and exciting thriller. The impact of the book is strong where the conclusion is already known to the writer and the subplots are also directed toward that finale. Your writing must similarly have an objective in mind from the outset.

Advantages of keeping the overall purpose in mind

- Recommendations, and the arguments leading to them, are matched. Your writing goes through the logical steps of identifying the problem, examining the problem, analyzing the results of the examination, drawing conclusions and making sensible recommendations.
- The writing will have a clear direction and greater impact. It will carry readers along, springing no surprises. They should be fully aware throughout of the direction the writing is taking.
- You are focused on the job at hand and have a clear, concise goal in mind.
- You have the big picture as a directive throughout the writing exercise. This means that besides the material of the exercise, you are aware of the wider impact the writing will have.
- Starting at the end highlights any gaps in your reasoning. If, when writing, you do not know where you are heading then you cannot expect to see any omissions in the work. If you are clear as to the general direction, then weaknesses in arguments or research can easily be identified and corrected.

Disadvantages of having the big picture in mind throughout

- Having the overall purpose in mind can lead to rigid thinking, so that having determined the end result, you will fail to see effective alternatives.
- It can also lead to cheating. Having determined the answer, it is possible for you to bend, modify, or select facts that support your argument and ignore, or give lesser weight, to those that do not. There is obviously a conflict between having a commitment to the subject of the writing and being open to alternatives. This conflict should be resolved in the earlier, planning stage so that when you are writing you will have already resolved or catered to the conflict by an accepted compromise.

In the authors' opinion, the advantages of not writing until you have the overall purpose in mind far outweigh the disadvantages.

Think it out in advance

There are several steps to organizing your thinking before writing a report.

First, gather together all the information needed for your writing and store it in one place. Depending on the scope of the project, you may need just a single file, a filing cabinet drawer, or even a whole filing cabinet. The larger the project, the more organized and subdivided even the filing of the basic data must be, so that it can be retrieved easily. At this stage, however, you are only concerned with making sure that you have all the information in one place and in useful order. When you begin putting your document together, you should not have to sift through a host of irrelevant information.

Second, arrange the information into an outline format, to show information relating to:

- why the document was commissioned;
- methods of research used;
- research undertaken;
- findings;
- conclusions;
- recommendations.

Bear in mind that you are not yet writing the document but merely organizing the information you have collected into these various subheadings. If any gaps become apparent, then carry out the necessary further research before developing the writing further.

Your writing will be appreciated through the eyes only

Consider why you look in the mirror to adjust your tie, put on makeup, comb your hair, or whatever. Why do you check up on your appearance? Isn't it because you want to make a particular impression on others, and because you want to feel good about yourself? In effect, you are putting yourself on display. You are dressing your store window. It is the outside of you that people see first, and you want to make a good impression.

In writing, it is vital to remember that no matter how thorough the research, how logically presented the argument, how clever you as the writer are, it is the writing that must make the good impression, for many of your readers will see nothing more of you than the document you produce. In the end, they may be persuaded by the force of your argument alone, but do not rely on that; make sure that the appearance of your writing is attractive, and the style easy to follow.

Techniques of persuasion

For your report to be persuasive, you need to employ certain techniques.

Identify the big message. Your writing must make clear its main aims, conclusions, and recommendations. They must be spelled out without ambiguity. A document with a clear message is more effective than one either with no main points or with its main points hidden.

You must sell your writing. Readers will be looking for what's in it for them. Tell them what is in it for them, stressing the advantages of them doing what you want them to do.

Get the selling points up front. Don't be afraid to put your selling points up front. It is not something to be embarrassed about, and there is little point in not selling boldly. The salesman who is shy to sell makes very few sales.

Be aware of the readers' bias toward the material. The reader or readers may already have a viewpoint about the recommendations you are making. A little homework in discovering this viewpoint will enable you to present the material in a way likely to be well received. If you are seeking a particular course of action from the reader, then you are more likely to get it if you address any reservations the reader has.

How does the reader see you? The way your reader will receive your work will depend on how the reader views you. Does he or she trust you? Are you known for doing thorough work or sloppy work? Are your views thought to be well weighted or heavily biased? It is not easy to ask these questions of yourself, but the more you know yourself, and the way you are perceived, the more you can predict responses to your work.

Your arguments must be well balanced to keep your writing from looking one-sided. Even though you should have, and demonstrate, your passion toward your writing, it should contain well-balanced presentations of alternatives. If your writing leaves out other possibilities, it will appear—and be—one-sided. The reader will have to seek out the alternatives for himself or herself, and you will have failed to impress the reader with your research.

Get the reader to a state of agreement and compliance. Your reader will need to be persuaded that there is a case for agreeing with your proposals. To put that case logically, it is necessary to go through six simple stages in your writing (that summarize points made earlier):

- The hook. Get your readers' attention by pointing out the advantages to them; to their career, their finances, their status, and so on.
- Explain the problem. Explain the situation as it was, and how the problem arose. Move from the historic to the present day, and from the general to the specific, so that the reader is carried along logically and is able to understand the problem as you see it.
- Offer your solution to the problem. Be sure to cover alternative solutions and state why you think your recommendation is the best one. If you believe your reader will have questions or difficulties with these suggestions, anticipate them and address them.
- Justify any costs. This will anticipate a common challenge to recommendations—expense.
- Show that your suggestions are workable, preferably by giving examples of where they have worked in other, similar, situations.

- Describe the situation as it will be after your recommendations have been implemented so that the reader can understand the difference that you propose to make.

The next step

Tell your readers what you want from them: agreement, action, a recommendation to higher authority, and so on. Make it clear what your readers' next step is after reading your document. Too often written presentations fail at this point because readers are unsure of their role as seen by the writer.

The order of writing
(which is not the order of presentation)

When you have planned the first draft of the report, you can use the following as a guideline approach to its creation.

- Draft the end of the report first because, as stated earlier, before actually drafting the report you must be committed to the end conclusions and recommendations, by virtue of the thorough work already carried out. Thus focused, the report will have greater cohesion and higher impact.
- Draft the expansions of conclusions. That is, working backward through the report, and having drafted the conclusions, draft the more detailed reasons why you arrived at those conclusions.
- Draft the introduction, stating why the report was undertaken. Before you get into the detail of the main body, it should here become clear to you whether the end conclusions are a reasonable product of the initial reason the report was undertaken. If they are not, then some gaps in logic have probably not been identified. Rethink through the work.
- Draft the main body and appendices of the report. This is the point when all of the relevant information on file is summarized into your first draft of the report.
- Decide upon the title of your report unless this has already been dictated to you by those commissioning the report. Remember, the title is the first selling point of a report and is the only part read by 100 percent of readers. Make it punchy, interesting, and instantly attractive to the reader. If the title is drafted at the beginning, there is a tendency to direct the work—and eventually the report itself—toward the title, thus putting the cart before the horse. The report is the fundamentally important thing; the title is simply the first selling point of the complete presentation.

Physical appearance of your report

To make your report easy on the eyes, consider the following guidelines.

Use 8½ × 11-inch paper. It is a standard for business use and feels right. Smaller sheets of paper can get lost in in-trays; larger sheets annoy people because they don't fit into files and get torn and worn when they overlap or jut out of files too small for them.

Have a separate cover with a descriptive title, your name as the author, the date of the report, and the circulation list of the report. Don't clutter it up with anything else. Keep it simple; keep it smart.

For longer reports, or reports with many sections, provide a contents page. There should also be effective cross-referencing throughout to make the report easy to use. Remember that it is not always the first reading of the report that counts—thorough though that is likely to be. Once read, a good report should allow the reader easy reaccess without the need to think, "Now where did I see that particular item?"

Start each main heading at the top of a new page. Cramped presentation reflects cramped thinking and invites cramped appreciation. Give your report light and air, and the reader will be all the more receptive and creative in reading it. This presentation also allows you to reorder, amend, or insert material without disturbing other sections.

Be consistent with headings and subheadings. For example, consider putting all main headings in the center of the line, and keeping subheadings flush with the left-hand margin. The decision you take on what to do is not as crucial as keeping consistency. The style of presentation must feel comfortable to the reader; an inconsistent layout will irritate.

Make sure that the information under each heading relates to that heading. When you move on to another topic, start it with a new heading. This will make it easier for your readers to find their way around your report.

Do not overload your report with underscoring, boldface, italics, and so on. It looks clumsy and disagreeable to the eye. Where possible, keep to boldface, perhaps some underscoring. If you need—or want—to use italics, do so in substitution for one of the others. Keep print size consistent, with variations only for headings.

Allow generous margins all around the page. Leave at least 1½ inches on the left-hand side so that even when the report is fastened into a file, the words at the left-hand margin will not be fastened through or buried under the fold of the paper. Leave at least 1 inch to the right, and more if you want to allow space for yourself or others to make marginal notations. Leave 1 inch minimum at the top and bottom of the page.

In the presentation of each page, use plenty of white space. These gaps between paragraphs, headings, sections, and so on have an important psychological effect on the reader. Each block of type is easily absorbed and the eyes are allowed to rest before moving on to the next paragraph and the next concept. White space also creates patterns in the blocks of type that make the page look interesting and exciting, avoiding the monotonous and crowded effect of solid pages of type. Following this section (page 134) is a page with no white space. See how uncomfortable it is to read that page and how much more difficult it is to absorb the information.

Present the report in double spacing—or at the very least one and a half times spacing—and on one side of the paper only.

Number every page, preferably using a notation such as 1/23, 2/23, and so on (in other words, page one of twenty-three, page two of twenty-three), so that the reader knows not only the page number but also the total number of pages in the report. This makes it easy to check that there are no missing pages. Number even the front cover, and then nothing can go astray.

Always keep a file copy. If the original is in electronic form (stored by a word processor), then keep a backup of the disk. Also make a hard copy (a printout).

Personal Presentations to Assist Reports

The basic rule for making a presentation of a written document is not to present the writing by reading it to its recipients. Your readers can read your documents in their own time and in their own way. The purpose of your presentation is not to give the document but rather to sell its main points and recommendations.

- Consider the production of attractive colorful transparencies, overhead projector slides, and graphics to illustrate your main points.
- Prepare slides of key supporting points of the writing, but not detailed paragraphs. Use the slides as reminder notes for you to make an informal and verbal presentation of the key points.
- If there are key photographs or artists' illustrations involved, have these enlarged into displays and arrange them around the presentation room.
- If training or other illustrative video material can be used to emphasize certain points, then arrange to give a small video presentation.
- Encourage interaction and debate to enliven people's interest in the report and increase their personal feeling of involvement.
- Make sure that your presentation is physically comfortable for the audience (comfortable chairs, a well-lit spacious room, and so on).

SAMPLE PAGE WITHOUT WHITE SPACE: To make your report easy on the eyes, consider the following guidelines. Use 8½ x 11-inch paper. It is a standard for business use and feels right. Smaller sheets of paper can get lost in in-trays; larger sheets annoy people because they don't fit into files and get torn and worn when they overlap or jut out of files too small for them. Have a separate cover with a descriptive title, your name as the author, the date of the report, and the circulation list of the report. Don't clutter it up with anything else. Keep it simple; keep it smart. For longer reports, or reports with many sections, provide a contents page. There should also be effective cross-referencing throughout to make the report easy to use. Remember that it is not always the first reading of the report that counts—thorough though that is likely to be. Once read, a good report should allow the reader easy reaccess without the need to think, "Now where did I see that particular item?" Start each main heading at the top of a new page. Cramped presentation reflects cramped thinking and invites cramped appreciation. Give your report light and air, and the reader will be all the more receptive and creative in reading it. This presentation also allows you to reorder, amend, or insert material without disturbing other sections. Be consistent with headings and subheadings. For example, consider putting all main headings in the center of the line, and keeping subheadings flush with the left-hand margin. The decision you take on what to do is not as crucial as keeping consistency. The style of presentation must feel comfortable to the reader; an inconsistent layout will irritate. Make sure that the information under each heading relates to that heading. When you move on to another topic, start it with a new heading. This will make it easier for your readers to find their way around your report. Do not overload your report with underscoring, boldface, italics, and so on. It looks clumsy and disagreeable to the eye. Where possible, keep to boldface, perhaps some underscoring. If you need—or want—to use italics, do so in substitution for one of the others. Keep print size consistent, with variations only for headings. Allow generous margins all around the page. Leave at least 1½ inches on the left-hand side so that even when the report is fastened into a file, the words at the left-hand margin will not be fastened through or buried under the bend of the paper. Leave at least 1 inch to the right, and more if you want to allow space for yourself or others to make marginal notations. Leave 1 inch minimum at the top and bottom of the page. In the presentation of each page, use plenty of white space. These gaps between paragraphs, headings, sections, and so on have an important psychological effect on the reader. Each block of type is easily absorbed and the eyes are allowed to rest before moving on to the next paragraph and the next concept. White space also creates patterns in the blocks of type that make the page look interesting and exciting, avoiding the monotonous and crowded effect of solid pages of type. Following this section is a page with no white space. See how uncomfortable it is to read that page and how much more difficult it is to absorb the information. Present the report in double spacing—or at the very least one and a half times spacing and on one side of the paper only. Number every page, preferably using a notation such as 1/23, 2/23, and so on (in other words, page one of twenty-three, page two of twenty-three), so that the reader knows not only the page number but also the total number of pages in the report. This makes it easy to check that there are no missing pages. Number even the front cover, and then nothing can go astray. Always keep a file copy. If the original is in electronic form (stored by a word processor), then keep a backup of the disk. Also make a hard copy (a printout). Cross-referencing and numbering: Depending on the report type you may number virtually every paragraph. If so, make sure that the contents lists them in a descriptive way and that the cross-referencing is consistent throughout. It may be a rash comment, and there is bound to be someone who will prove us wrong, but the general rule in reports is that you cannot overdo the referencing. Replace words with pictures. Consider whether some of the text can be replaced by pictures, illustrations, diagrams, and photographs. In fact, much of this should have been organized along the way and should have been falling into place as your writing was assembled. If you decide to use illustrations, budget for the time and other resources necessary to acquire them. It may be that a photographer has to be engaged or that a desktop publishing program will be necessary. One report examined by the authors of this book spent considerable time describing the appearance of stress and strain marks in worn-out metal.

How to make sure that your presentation is effective

Be sure to leave yourself plenty of time to plan the presentation and time for others to provide you with information, illustrative material, and photographs.

Rehearse your presentation so that you understand it. You should be fully conversant with all the material so that you can deliver it in an informal style. This will allow you to discuss wider implications raised by the audience.

Talk to people outside the meeting before the presentation and become aware of current informal discussions and political implications regarding the presentation you are going to make. Respond by anticipating difficulties and allaying preconceived fears in the audience's mind.

Present as many facts as possible, but in a lively and varied way so that the presentation continues to be interesting. Unsupported ideas can be challenged and can appear as a lack of professionalism on your part in the minds of the audience. It may be that you have the facts to support your arguments but if you present the arguments without the facts you will make your case look all the weaker.

Before you go into the presentation, know what impact you want to have so that you can target your audience accordingly. If you are presenting a subject of serious concern, then make sure that the presentation reflects that seriousness. If appropriate, inject a degree of humor to turn a subject people are avoiding into one that people are prepared to deal with.

Consider the alternative proposals and opposition that you will receive and prepare your counterarguments for the most obvious of them. That does not mean that you can be expected to anticipate every possibility, but the more you can counter, the more you will be seen to have understood and prepared your material well. You will be seen to be in command of your subject.

Remember that well-prepared arguments are never exposed as wrong. Others may have better ideas but usually there are only choices between alternatives, rarely right and wrong ideas. If you have researched your work well, then you will be presenting a valid alternative. If a better alternative is suggested, and you become persuaded of this, then accept this gracefully and show support for the better idea.

Do not try to monopolize the presentation. Where possible, make it interactive with the audience. Certainly it is your presentation and you can set the tone, but do not prevent others having their say. If you do this, they will have their discussion without you after the presentation and alternatives will be developed that you are not a party to. You will lose the initiative on a subject where, currently, you are regarded as the expert.

Practice basic presentation techniques. These are outside the scope of this book but include:

- practicing fluent speaking to avoid blank-outs, excessive "hmms" and "aahs," and other irritating mannerisms;
- avoiding the need to shuffle papers by having your key words on slides behind you;

- speaking slowly and clearly—do not get excited and flustered, keeping yourself calm using rhythmic and regular breathing;
- using vocal and other expressions that add color and dimension to your presentation—but be wary of gestures that can sometimes offend.

Never bluff. If you do not have the facts on hand, then admit that and promise to obtain them and report back when practical. If you try to bluff, then you may be found out and the attitude of the audience toward you will be one of suspicion.

Be enthusiastic. Enthusiasm is contagious and exciting for everyone.

Advantages of personal presentations

- A personal presentation allows for message adjustment. If you feel that the audience is not with you, you can adjust your style, emphasize points that you believe have not been properly received, and so on.
- A personal presentation is interactive. It allows for feedback and for development of ideas by the inclusion of other people's contributions.
- The presenter can use body language and eye contact to emphasize certain points: to stress what is significant. It also allows for morale building and motivation in a team, in that the presenter can use the powerful communicative techniques of smiling, winking, laughing, and so on, all of which are often understood far better than the written word.
- The presenter is able to receive the body language of others and thereby determine the impact she is having.
- The audience can ask for clarification when they don't understand something. Written reports can leave people thirsty for knowledge when a particular point is not fully explained.
- A personal presentation is less permanent and can allow a person to be more forthright in delivery or explanation. There is a tendency to hold back extreme passion when committing to writing.

Exercise 13
Making a presentation. Take a recent document you wrote or received and find radical ways to present some of the information in a presentation. Be creative; let your imagination run wild as you design a presentation that will have high impact.

Exercise 14
Toning-up exercises to work out your writing skills.

Exercise 14a
Describe the drawing below in words.

Exercise 14b
Read the following passage once. Then cover up the passage and do not refer to it when answering the questions.

The checkout assistant had just closed out the cash register and put a "closed" sign across the aisle when a masked woman appeared and ordered the assistant to hand over all the money in the register. The owner opened the register. The money was taken out and the masked woman ran away. The assistant telephoned the police.

Questions
1. Did the masked person appear before or after the assistant had closed out the cash register?
2. What did the assistant do after closing out the register?
3. What sex was the masked person?
4. Did the masked person demand money?
5. Did the assistant hand over the money?
6. Did the store owner telephone the police?
7. What sex was the assistant?
8. How many people were involved in the incident?
9. Did the owner put a "closed" sign across the aisle?
10. Who took the money out of the register?
11. How did the masked person leave?
12. What kind of place did this incident happen in?

Now check your answers with the passage. Some of the questions test only your comprehension and will be either right or wrong. Other questions test the degree to which you create facts that are not there from the world as you know it. ➤

Particular points to consider:

(a) In order to visualize the action, the reader will often create an image; the danger is that the image so created becomes a memory. For example, the sex of the owner is never stated. Did you impose a sex in your mind's eye?

(b) People often impose stereotypes in vague situations. Again, there is a danger that the creation becomes a memory. For example, the sex of the assistant is never stated, yet many people automatically assume that a checkout assistant will be female. (There are many such examples in our everyday life: all nurses are women; all doctors are men, and so on.)

(c) Some facts are missing, yet are needed for a proper understanding of the situation. The same danger of imposed memory applies. For example, it is easy to assume that this incident took place in a food supermarket because that is where checkout aisles are most commonly seen. However, this is never stated in the passage.

Exercise 14c

Examining the following list of items and classify them in suitable categories. (They are typical complaints about the stresses of going on vacation by plane.)

- I went to Spain, but my luggage went to Greece.
- There is far too much waiting time at the departure airport.
- All we could get in the departure airport was stale sandwiches.
- Every flight was delayed. No one ever told us what was causing the delays to our schedule.
- The cabins were too full of luggage sticking out into the aisles.
- Our suitcases were scratched and split when we recovered them.
- It was never clear which gate we had to board through.
- There was not enough legroom between the plane seats.
- We were unable to specify that we wanted window seats.
- We had to take what we were given.
- No one at the departure airport seemed to know what was happening from one minute to the next.
- The bathrooms in the destination airport were dirty.
- The destination airport restaurant was shut.
- The plane had no smoking section.
- The bathrooms in our area were closed; we had to go to another terminal building while waiting for departure.
- I like to smoke a pipe and the stewardess would not let me.
- There were not enough seats in the departure lounges. We ended up sitting on the floor.
- The food on the plane was tasteless. ➤

- The seats were too uncomfortable for a long trip.
- I was unable to get a vegetarian meal on the plane.
- Bad scheduling meant I had to spend hours in one airport waiting for my connection.
- The airport where we waited to change planes was too hot and stuffy.
- We were sent to the wrong departure gate because no one told the staff about a last-minute change.
- I could never get to the airplane bathrooms because the aisle was always jammed with carts serving food, drinks, and duty-free goods.
- The paperwork seemed unnecessary; the tickets had to be exchanged for boarding passes instead of doubling for that role.
- We were directed to another airport on arrival, but no one offered us an apology.
- There were no buses to meet us at the new destination airport after we were rerouted. We had to wait hours.
- The lighting was too bright to enjoy looking out of the window on the night flights.

These points could be classified in many ways. For example,

(a) According to location: departure airport, airplane, departure airport, destination airport.
(b) According to blame: airport staff, airplane staff, general administration, and so on.

Practice the logic of classifying facts. It will help you to order your thinking when the time comes to report on a large project or assignment.

Exercise 14d – Spider diagram exercises

Imagine that you are about to do the following tasks. Design spider diagrams that will help you to plan your work. The aim is to make it more probable that you will complete the tasks efficiently, leaving nothing important out and duplicating no effort.

(a) Tidy up your office paperwork.
(b) Spring clean your home.
(c) Write a film script.
(d) Buy a new home.
(e) Learn to be a good amateur photographer.
(f) Bake a cake.
(g) Choose and install a new computer system for your office (and learn to use it!).
(h) Plan an evening out for you and a friend.
(i) Redesign a garden.
(j) Make a dining room table.

Use the spider diagram on page 93 as a guide. Remember to develop a style that suits you.

Exercise 14e

Take any written work: a report, a novel, a reference book, and so on. Try to find as many exciting images as you can to replace chunks of the text. This is a useful thinking process to learn, and stops you from becoming bogged down in complicated descriptions without realizing the potential for illustration.

PART 4

Assertiveness

One of the most popular training courses we have held in inter-personal skills over recent years has been in assertiveness. Many secretaries have recognized that they fail to present themselves as they should do, fail to stand up for their natural rights and fail to establish satisfying personal and working relationships.

There are many misconceptions about assertiveness training. Many delegates have told us that their bosses wish them well for the course but warn them: "Don't think this means you can come back here bossing me around." Assertiveness training is not about bossing other people around. By the same token, we have always recognized that probably of those who need our assertiveness training courses, most never get on them; they are the people who are too reticent to put their names forward to their bosses for the course!

Many assertiveness courses rely on building up your beliefs in yourself, asking you to see yourself in a different light, or asking you to rethink the way you view the world. This is all well and good and for some people is an effective approach. However, the most common complaint that we have heard from people on our courses, often people who have been on other courses that have not worked for them, is "I felt very good when I had finished the course but I was still faced with the dilemma, what is it I do tomorrow that is different from what I did today?" We sympathize. Going to work tomorrow feeling different about yourself does nothing about the situations and circumstances that you faced yesterday and that you will continue to face. Our course is very practical, interrupting the belief–behavior loop at a different point.

Belief–Behavior Feedback Loop

Your beliefs, opinions, attitudes, and values

lead to . . .

The rights you believe you have, and the rights you believe others have

lead to . . .

The way you behave (what you do and what you say)

leads to . . .

Your view of the world (and your place in it)

leads to . . .

A feedback to your beliefs, opinions, attitudes, and values.

The belief–behavior feedback loop works in the following way:

- *Your beliefs, opinions, attitudes, and values* are based on your observations and experiences of the world as you have grown up in it. They come from a variety of sources, which we shall examine later. The beliefs that you hold dictate . . .
- *The rights you believe are yours, and the rights you allow others.* We shall examine below the natural rights in work and in everyday life that you are entitled to. However, many people do not recognize these as rights or would even deny that they are right because of the beliefs they hold. The rights you allow yourself and the rights you attribute to others will dictate . . .
- *Your behavior: what you do and what you say.* Based on your view of yourself and other people, you will behave in a certain way. Behavior is very important as it is the only aspect of people that is visible to others. No matter what you believe, no matter what you think, no matter what values you hold dear, people can only form opinions about you from their observations. The behavior of assertive people is consistent with their beliefs about themselves and others; the behavior of nonassertive or aggressive people is often inconsistent as it seeks in many ways to be manipulative. People will respond to your behavior and this will lead you to analyze . . .
- *Your view of the world and your place in it.* The way you act will create responses in people around you and you will observe those responses. The responses of others to your behavior will change or reinforce . . .
- *Your beliefs* . . . and so on.

Conventional training suggests that you change your beliefs first, and rethink the rights you give yourself and others; that this will lead to a change in behavior; that the change in behavior will affect your interpretation of the world and that this will reinforce your new beliefs. However, for most people this is a short-term effect and within weeks you find yourself acting as you used to. Greater success comes from interrupting the belief–behavior feedback loop at the point of behavior. Change your behavior, watch people's responses to your changed behavior, and you will automatically reinforce or change your beliefs, based on practical observation and what amounts to experimentation. This will reinforce or change your view of the rights to which you and others are entitled and this will further modify or reinforce your behavior. This form of interruption in the belief–behavior loop has a longer-lasting, even permanent, effect.

Both authors of this book have been involved in many practical examples of this in training programs in major U.K. companies over the past 10 to 15 years. One particular example has always stood out in our minds. One of the authors was part of a team of some 20 trainers delivering a year-long program to a London City finance organization that was designed to develop management ability in the group. The first practical delivery was presentation skills. Part of the day consisted of the delegates each giving a five-minute presentation, which was video recorded, and against which they could compare their performances as they developed throughout the day and throughout the program over the year.

Susan has to have been the most inhibited and incapable presenter to appear in a training room. She tried to resist giving her presentation at all despite her colleagues having done so, her speech became both inaudible and unintelligible, and she misused all the equipment, including standing in front of the overhead projector and projecting her slides onto her own face. She flustered, went red, and eventually shook her head, held her throat to indicate she simply could not talk, and walked away.

We did not try to teach her to believe in her abilities or to understand that her colleagues fully supported her. We taught her practical presentation skills, awareness of equipment, awareness of space around her, tricks like wearing clothes without pockets so that she had nowhere to hide her hands, and so on. Even in the space of this one day, by making a more effective presentation (i.e., changing her behavior) she was able to see for herself the very genuine support she was getting from her colleagues and their very genuine appreciation of her newly acquired skills. This in turn created firm beliefs that she could do it if she wanted to, which encouraged her to continue; she had therefore permanently modified her behavior. She now felt that she was more competent in presentation delivery.

This would be a very small victory, and a very common one, if this was all that was entailed. However, over the course of the whole year, many subjects were delivered on a practical skills base and Susan, like the other delegates, made behavioral changes and observed the results of those changes. They were observing them not only in their workplace and among their colleagues, but in the wider company as a whole and indeed in their everyday life. The broad range of skills acquired showed very clearly in their highly successful career tracks, which involved accelerated promotion, and many of them commented on the positive influence the training had brought to their personal relationships with others outside of work.

Two aspects of Susan's success are notable. First, she was part of the presentation of the course to the following year's potential candidates. All of the current year's group had to take the stand in an auditorium, with an audience of some 100 people, including their managers, potential candidates for the next year, the training teams, and so on. Susan acted as master of ceremonies for the day and presented the whole day's "stage show" with the skill of a professional. Second, she told me privately that one very pleasing effect of the training was that she could now complain in stores when she felt she was not being given the service or goods she wanted. She had never felt able to complain before.

An important point about the story is that nowhere in the course was there specifically assertiveness training. The assertiveness was automatically acquired from using the skills that had been learned and observing other people's reactions to those skills. And the change seems to have been permanent: a confidence–promotion–additional skills–confidence cycle that continues for Susan and for all the delegates on the various years' courses to date.

What Are Your Rights?

Assertiveness includes standing up for yourself and your rights, but in a way that respects others. You cannot defend your rights unless you have some idea of what they include.

- The right to your own beliefs, opinions, attitudes, and values.
- The right to change your mind.
- The right to make mistakes.
- The right not to know or understand something.

How frequently do people take instructions for tasks without fully understanding them but feeling it would somehow be inappropriate to ask for information they somehow feel they should know. How often do people sit in training sessions and let something they do not understand pass by them without challenging it, often not realizing that everyone else in the room is in the same position? There is no failure on your part in not knowing something, only a failure in not seeking to find it out.

- The right to express both positive and negative emotions.
- The right not to get involved in someone else's problems if you do not want to.
- The right to say "no" at appropriate times.
- The right to be your own conscience and suffer your own consequences.
- The right not to have to act to please others.
- The right to ask others to respect your rights.

This is not an exhaustive list. Your human rights could be summed up as being your right to anything provided that your rights respect the rights of others.

We might further summarize rights that relate to your job. Many of your human rights are the same but there are specific areas relating to your job:

- The right to know the level of performance expected from you.
- The right to know what your appraisals have indicated.
- The right to know your objectives.
- The right to make mistakes.
- The right to contribute to the choice of your team.
- The right to agree on performance levels with your team or staff.
- The right to criticize the performance of staff when standards fall below agreed levels (see Giving and Receiving Criticism page 183).
- The right to be involved in matters that affect you, your work, and your promotion.
- The right to make decisions about things that concern your workplace.

One delegate on a training course told us that she worked in an open plan office where everyone had identical workstations and workstation layouts. She had asked for permission to put a small potted plant on her workstation; this was refused on the grounds that "it would make your workstation different from everyone else's and that is not allowed." Such trivial matters should not even be the cause of having to assert your rights, but there are many times when it is appropriate that you need to be involved in decisions about your workplace.

- The right to say "no" at appropriate times.

Again this list cannot be exhaustive and your rights should be restricted only by your obligation to respect the rights of others.

Exercise 15 – How assertive are you?

Circle the number most appropriate to each statement.

	Never				Always
When I show my anger, I do not blame others.	1	2	3	4	5
I do not have problems expressing my feelings.	1	2	3	4	5
I am comfortable speaking to groups of people.	1	2	3	4	5
I have no anxiety asking others to do tasks.	1	2	3	4	5
I can say "no" easily.	1	2	3	4	5
I can express my honest opinions to my boss.	1	2	3	4	5
I can show my disagreement with others.	1	2	3	4	5
When the behavior of others becomes a problem for me, I can express this easily.	1	2	3	4	5
I accept the beliefs of others openly and without criticism.	1	2	3	4	5
My rights are as important as those of others.	1	2	3	4	5
I accept new tasks without anxiety.	1	2	3	4	5
I trust others and believe people are basically competent.	1	2	3	4	5
I can delegate tasks effectively.	1	2	3	4	5
I acknowledge my mistakes easily.	1	2	3	4	5
I have no problem meeting new people.	1	2	3	4	5

Score and appraisal

15–30: You are not very assertive. Generally you show signs of nonassertion, probably to avoid conflict with others. Success in applying even a few areas of this chapter will increase the quality of your life at home and at work.

31–45: You can be assertive when you consciously think about it but your instinctive reaction is too often to act aggressively or nonassertively. This chapter will direct your attention to those areas where you can begin to become more instinctively assertive. ➤

46–60: You are basically assertive. There may be times when your instincts fail you and you become nonassertive or aggressive, but these are probably few and far between. There is room for improving your natural assertiveness.

61–75: Your are assertive and handle situations effectively. You are in control of your life at home or work, and you relate to others well. This chapter will contain development points for you, but will be mostly useful in giving you assistance in developing the assertiveness of others.

You should not think that this represents a permanent view of your assertiveness. You should go through the questionnaire once every six months and, assuming you are working on your assertiveness using principles set out in this chapter, you should see your score increasing.

Outcomes of Assertiveness

This chapter assumes that increased assertiveness is a good thing. We believe that it is but for specific reasons. Assertive people invariably display the following characteristics.

Increased confidence in themselves. Assertive people seem to walk taller, act more calmly, and speak with greater authority.

Ability to trust and have confidence in others. We have many case histories from our training courses of people who were able to delegate to others as a result of their being able to let go of the reins, and as a result were selected for promotion in their companies.

Increased self-responsibility. The confidence of assertiveness allows people to accept greater responsibility, knowing that they will live up to it.

Greater time management successes. By refusing improper requests assertively (saying "no" when appropriate), assertive people do not let others solve their time management problems at their expense. As the section on time management in these books indicates, a significant part of time management involves preventing others from using you unfairly.

Ability to take the initiative. Assertive people are not afraid of failure. They see such negative outcomes as a learning experience. They are ready to explain what risks were taken and why, and ready to accept the consequences of lack of success. From this, they are people who create or build genuine successes.

Their needs are met. By expressing your needs, wants, and desires in a direct and honest manner, you create an environment where they are more likely to be met.

They exert a positive influence over others. In boss–secretary partnerships, assertive secretaries have greater success in getting their bosses to respect their side of that partnership.

They have control over their own life. One delegate on a course told the group the story of her having offered to take a neighbor shopping in her car after the neighbor had been unable to drive. This had always been intended to be a short-term solution to the neighbor's problem but had been going on for over a year, long after the person had wanted to stop it. We received feedback following a one-day assertiveness course that she had followed our guidelines and not only brought this unhappy circumstance to an end but done so in a way that had in no way damaged her other ongoing relationships with her neighbors.

Characteristics of Behavior Patterns

There are four behavior patterns available in a situation: passive nonassertion, dismissive nonassertion, aggression, and assertion. The characteristics of these four behavior patterns are as follows.

Passive nonassertion

Passive nonassertive people do not stand up for their own rights. Where they do make an attempt to express their rights, they do so in a way that allows, or even encourages, others to downgrade them or treat them with reduced respect. Passive nonassertive people express their needs, desires, opinions, feelings, or convictions in apologetic ways, and are subliminally acknowledging their belief that other people's needs or wants are more important than their own.

Passive nonassertive people do not express themselves in direct, honest, and open ways. They devalue themselves and transmit the signal that they believe they have little or nothing to contribute of value to a situation.

People become nonassertive in order to avoid confrontation, conflict, or getting into a win–lose situation that they feel they will lose. Quite often passive nonassertive people are those who are seeking love or affection from others and are trying to please in order to gain that emotional response. They are, generally, insecure people.

Passive nonassertive people have developed a fear of failure and in order to avoid failure find excuses to prevent them from taking risks that could lead to further failure. They will find often irrational reasons for not taking on new tasks, such as "I am not very good with photocopiers, I'd rather not do that job." They make themselves losers at everyone else's expense, giving the risky jobs, which eventually lead to recognition and promotion, to others. As a consequence, they reinforce their own perception of themselves as failures because over time they can point out quite correctly that they seem to have failed continually, i.e., they have not been recognized or been promoted. Passively nonassertive people can be depressingly negative and stunt the risk-taking and creativity in others. Because they are unable to express themselves clearly, they will often allow small problems to become larger ones, or easily dealt with problems to simmer for ages, when a more open stance could put minor problems behind them easily.

Dismissive nonassertion

Dismissive nonassertive people have come to believe that others will automatically overrule their own rights, and they have become willing victims, subconsciously encouraging people to put them down.

Dismissive nonassertive people express their needs and wants in negative ways, assuming that they will be dismissed by others. They do not express themselves in honest and open ways but usually through sarcasm and occasional bursts of aggression. Their belief is based on a view that everyone is out to get them.

The aim of dismissive nonassertive people is, often at the subconscious level, to set up a lose–lose situation where, having decided that they are going to lose anyway, they are determined to bring others down with them. They are basically insecure people fighting a world they see as trying to put them down. Dismissive nonassertive people seem to demonstrate, at least more openly, a higher degree of paranoia than most.

Dismissive people, having decided they are losers, reinforce their self-image by producing poor work and failing to turn up for appointments punctually or well prepared. They often exhibit extreme symptoms of stress, such as excessive drinking, psychosomatic illness, and so on. Although nonassertive, their language can often be aggressive behind the backs of those they are condemning.

Aggression

Aggressive people are, of course, more able to stand up for their own rights but in doing so act in a way that downgrades or dismisses the rights of others. A quote famously attributed to Atilla the Hun is, "It is not enough that I win; everyone else must lose."

Aggressive people do not give consideration to the needs and wants of others. If they do meet the needs, wants, or desires of other people, it is usually because it suits their own ends. Aggressive people use inappropriate language and body language to express themselves, with a view to manipulating others into situations of advantage to the aggressor. They believe that their own needs and desires are of more importance than anyone else's; indeed, they either disregard or do not even think of the other person or people.

Aggressive people deliberately set up win–lose situations with the aim of winning at the expense of others. They do so because, like nonassertive people, they are insecure and express their insecurity in a need for power and victory.

The starting point for aggressive people is that they strongly believe that, because they have arranged the world the way they want it, usually through bullying, it is now the duty of the rest of the world to fall in line with them. Theirs is not an attitude of respect for others. They see themselves as fighting under the law of the jungle, where the strongest survive on the basis that they have found themselves to be, or made themselves, the strongest in the environment in which they work. Because aggressive people have an image that they are virtually perfect and it is the rest of the world that is out of step, they rarely see themselves as at fault. The problem is always with someone else. Because of this, they rarely take responsibility for their own actions but seek scapegoats to blame for problems or failures.

Assertion

Assertive people exhibit an inner strength that allows them to stand up for their own rights while at the same time seeking to address the rights of others appropriately.

Assertive people express themselves in direct, open, honest ways using appropriate and consistent language and body language. They acknowledge the value of contributions by others. They seek to avoid win–lose situations and to create situations where compromise can meet the requirements of all the parties, allowing constructive progress.

Assertive people accept responsibility for mistakes and for making changes. They see mistakes as a learning experience and view other people's mistakes in the same light, helping them toward a constructive outcome.

Types of Assertion

There are different types of, or levels of, assertion to be used in different circumstances, or sequences of assertion to escalate your insistence that others respect your rights.

Basic assertion

Basic assertion is characterized by simple, clear statements expressing your opinions or desires in a straightforward and open manner that can be easily understood by the person you are speaking to. Typical statements used in basic assertion are:

"I cannot change my holiday arrangements."

"I want to discuss my salary increase."

Basic assertion is very useful when you are giving people information or praise, offering compliments, or making your own position clear. It can be used very effectively when you initially raise an issue because any resistance can then be countered by moving along the assertion escalation (see the further levels of assertion below) or reemphasizing a point already made. In this latter instance, you may have moved on to more elaborate levels of assertion and it is something of a shock tactic to come back to basic assertion, which cuts out the more elaborate dialogue and once again lays bare the bones of your position.

Questioning assertion

As an alternative way of setting out on an assertive dialogue where basic assertion might not be appropriate, questioning assertion allows for questions or statements to be made to find out where the other person stands in relation to the situation. Examples of questioning assertion dialogue are:

"Are you concerned about this course of action?"

"I would like to hear your opinions on this."

Questioning assertion is a good way of making sure that when you speak or act in a way that stands up for your own rights, you will not be violating the rights of others. It will enable you to determine not only what you believe other people's rights should or should not be but also what they believe their rights should or should not be. Questioning assertion allows you to investigate what alternatives are available that would be agreeable to others. Questioning assertion is also useful in beginning to build solutions with other people; it emphasizes that you intend to be assertive and increases the likelihood that you can make the other person respond assertively, which means that he or she will be much easier to deal with.

Empathetic assertion

It is a cornerstone of assertion that in standing up for or acknowledging your own rights, you should be standing up for and acknowledging the rights of others. This is most clearly expressed by showing your empathy with others, i.e., using language that makes clear that in addition to acknowledging your own beliefs, opinions, and so on, you are also aware of the feelings and needs of others. It should be stressed that we are talking about empathy, which is a positive constructive force, and not sympathy, which is usually negative and leads to nonassertive behavior from both parties. Examples of empathetic assertion dialogue are:

"I know we are all tired. However, I would like us to continue working on this for another hour."

"I realize that you need an estimate on completion from me, but I would like to look at my progress dates in detail before I give you that."

Empathetic assertion is used as a means of avoiding or resolving conflicts. Conflict often arises because others do not know that we understand their position, particularly where circumstances force us to create or endure a situation that is not to their liking. The very fact that they are aware that we understand their position is often enough to pacify their potential aggression and lead them into a situation of assertive compromise. Empathetic assertion also ensures that we hold ourselves back from overreaction. In order to make sure that you express yourself clearly, take a pause for a brief time to make sure that you express your understanding of the other person's position clearly. That pause, that delay, is often enough to change your own expressions from being possibly aggressive to being assertive.

A cornerstone of empathetic assertion is to make sure that you listen properly to what other people are telling you. That means listening with your ears open, and not your mouth! Empathetic assertion must be straightforward and clear and should contain an expression of your own feelings and the course of action you want.

Discrepancy assertion

We are very often confused or angered, and potentially led into aggression, by discovering that there is a discrepancy between what we thought was going to happen or what we had agreed would happen and what is actually happening. Discrepancy assertion is a dialogue that enables us to express the discrepancy and our feelings about it, and should include a clear statement of how we want the situation to change in the future. Examples of discrepancy assertion dialogue are:

> *"At my interview I was told that computer backup was to be my main task. But lately I have been taken from that and asked to do filing. I would like it clarified where my priorities are seen to be."*

> *"When we discussed secretarial duties you indicated that I would be doing the report typing. Ever since that time, I have noticed that Mary is doing that work. I am still eager to do the report typing."*

Discrepancy assertion should be used to lead people into seeing the discrepancies between their own words and actions. Quite often we have to understand that people do not realize they are speaking and acting inconsistently, and discrepancy assertion can be used to point this out to them. Very often it becomes immediately clear to them and the path is paved for constructive dialogue toward the rectification of possible injustices.

Discrepancy assertion is the appropriate starting point for any debate about apparent discrepancies. It allows for the possibility that we may be misunderstanding the situation and that once we have explained the apparent discrepancy as we see it the other person is encouraged to explain the situation as he sees it and perhaps to point out why we have an imbalanced view. As an illustration, in the first example above it may be that you have been in the office for only two working days that week, that computer backup was given priority on the three days you were not there, and that the filing only seems to have priority because it has become urgent owing to the priority given to computer backup. There may be no intention for that apparent imbalance to continue; you have the incorrect perspective. By you setting out your views in this way, the person you are speaking to can respond in a polite and effective way, correcting your mistaken view, without giving offense or feeling that he is being pushed into a conflict.

Discrepancy assertion is also useful for avoiding blaming people for discrepancies that might turn out to be no more than misunderstandings. In the second example above, your perception might be right that Mary is now doing the report typing that you are eager to do. However, it may be that your boss has decided to try you out on certain other tasks with a possible view to promotion. It may be also that your boss did not feel it appropriate to make that clear to you as an unfulfilled promise of promotion could be demotivating. If you express yourself in the manner given above your boss is able to explain the discrepancy, showing that it is to your advantage. You will not then be in a position of being embarrassed for having thrown your full weight against a door that turned out to be open all the time.

Negative feelings assertion

There is no reason for you to tolerate a situation that has an undesirable effect on you and that possibly indicates that someone standing up for his or her own rights is not acknowledging yours. You have every right to make an assertive statement that shows the effect of someone's behavior on you. An example of negative feelings assertion is:

> "*When you fail to give me the estimates on time, the effect is that I have to work through my lunch hour in order to meet our department's deadlines. This is very disruptive for me. In the future, I want you to keep to the agreement we made.*"

Negative feelings assertion is often a follow-up to the earlier, lower levels of assertion. When you have already expressed yourself using basic and empathetic assertion, and possibly had to counter excuses or denials with discrepancy assertion, if the person continues to ignore your rights, then negative feelings assertion makes clear the feelings that have been aroused in you and that have forced you to bring the issue to his or her attention.

Outcome assertion

The final sanction in assertive dialogue is outcome assertion, i.e., statements that make clear to the person you are talking to the outcome that will arise if his behavior does not change. In order that it is assertive and not aggressive, any such statement must give the person you are speaking to a means to avoid unpleasant outcomes and build constructive outcomes with you. Examples of outcome assertion dialogue are:

> "*If you are late again, then I have no alternative but to give you a written warning.*"

> "*If your work does not improve, then I must report it to your supervisor. I would rather not have to do that.*"

When using outcome assertion remember that it will only be effective providing you are prepared to, and have the authority (clout) to, implement the indicated outcome. It should only be used as a last resort as there is very little going back from this position. Once a debate has reached outcome assertion, then there is very little effect in going back to basic assertion, empathetic assertion, or even discrepancy assertion.

In the first example on the previous page, there is a pure statement of outcome assertion. In the second example, there is the combining of this ultimate (outcome) assertion with basic assertion in the closing phrase "I would rather not have to do that."

Later, in the section Dealing with Aggression in Others (beginning on page 163), we will look at how these levels of assertion can be used as a ladder of escalation. It should also of course be borne in mind that different situations may require a different starting approach. Having said that, negative feelings assertion and outcome assertion should almost always be an escalated level rather than a starting point. The other four levels of assertion can all be starting points in individual circumstances.

Understanding Aggressive Behavior

If we are to understand assertive behavior and why it is to our advantage we should understand how and why people become seduced by the alternatives. The first of these is aggression.

Why people become aggressive

A cornered tiger

The majority of wild animals, when they are about to be captured or, even more clearly, when they perceive that their young are about to be captured or killed, go through all the rituals of aggression: snarling, growling, lashing out, and so on. Of course, if pushed far enough, such animals will eventually strike out in desperation. People often become aggressive when they feel threatened. In corporate life, feeling threatened can include believing that your job is about to be replaced by technology, believing that you are about to be replaced by someone else, believing that you are about to be passed over for promotion, and so on. In these circumstances, people have a tendency to exhibit aggression. Presumably the underlying message of such aggression is "Leave me alone, leave my job alone, give me promotion, and I won't attack you." This leads us to the next point.

Hit back first

Some people become aggressive on the basis that if they hit back first they will be given what they want and any redundancies or passings over for promotion will be applied to other people. Those who hit back first presumably discovered that bullying can produce desired outcomes, though we will later look at the difference between the short-term and long-term outcomes of aggression.

Overcompensation for earlier nonassertive behavior

Quite often some typically trivial task becomes the straw that broke the camel's back. You may have accepted (possibly improperly) doing the photocopying job for months on end and all the time you have been bottling up a desire to refuse the task. Knowing that you have been nonassertive in accepting the task when you should not have done so, you reach that moment when you strike back at the person giving you the job. You immediately switch from nonassertive behavior to aggressive behavior in what you see as a last ditch attempt to defend your rights. This is of course a shock to the person you are dealing with because she is acting consistently and in a manner that has apparently had your approval (remember what we said at the beginning of this section, that behavior is the only part of us that is visible to others).

In one of our training courses, a secretary outlined a situation she had found intolerable. Despite the fact that she was fairly senior, her boss apparently believed that it was his secretary's job to peel his oranges for his lunch for him. She had done this for some months, all the time knowing that she felt unhappy with the situation. She asked whether, when she went back to work after our course, she should refuse to peel his oranges. We pointed out that a refusal would be aggressive. He was acting consistently and with permission given to him by her actions. It would also be nonassertive for her to continue doing something that she felt was inappropriate and that we agreed did not seem to respect her self-worth. The assertive solution was that when next asked to peel the orange, she should agree to do so but at the same time say something like, "I realize that I have previously accepted the job of peeling your oranges, but I should like to point out to you that this is not a job I believe I should be doing. I would like to hear your opinions on this and have the opportunity to discuss it with you." (We later heard that the outcome was as foreseen: her boss had never seen it as part of her job but it was a situation they had both fallen into; he had no objection to acknowledging that it was inappropriate for either of them to believe it was part of her job to peel his oranges and the matter was resolved very positively. When she does now peel his oranges, it is given and received in the spirit of a good-natured gift rather than a duty.)

Out-of-balance responses to previous experiences
Sometimes people become aggressive for quite inappropriate reasons resulting from often unconnected circumstances. For example, you might find that your regular parking space has been taken by another secretary, causing you to park some considerable distance from the entrance to your work premises. When you hear that that person has made some fairly minor mistake in, say, some typing, you might respond, "I'm not really surprised. She is a stupid woman at the best of times." She may well be a very effective typist and your response is based entirely on the unconnected circumstances in the parking lot causing you to feel aggressive toward her and express your feeling inappropriately at a given opportunity.

Exaggerating a problem in your own mind
Consider the following situation. You are walking toward your boss's office; he has asked you to come in because of a problem with a member of your staff. On the way to his office, you are saying to yourself, "I know what he is like; he enjoys moaning. I've got plenty of work to do and I'm not going to waste my time being hauled over the coals like this."

Your feelings throughout this walk toward your boss's office are anger, impatience, and frustration. As a result, when you arrive at your boss's office your defenses are up. Your anger is preventing you from hearing your boss effectively and your impatience and frustration force you to keep interrupting the boss, creating in him the impression that you do not care about the complaint, are not interested in his views, and are only concerned to defend yourself.

This all arises because you prejudged events, exaggerating them in your mind before they happened and programming yourself to act aggressively on arriving at the boss's office. The solution is to make sure that you count to ten and think before you act. Challenge your own preconceptions. For example, is "He enjoys moaning" fair? Does he really moan without reason and all that often? Or take "I'm not going to be hauled over the coals like this." Like what? Remember that you haven't even started the meeting yet and the hauling over the coals you are currently getting is entirely in your own mind.

As a final indignity, you might arrive at your boss's office, slam open the door, and impatiently say, "Right. What's all this about a problem with my staff? I haven't got all day to waste on this." And your boss might respond by saying, in an annoyed manner, "I wanted to point out that I was aware of the problem with your staff member and I was particularly pleased with the way you handled it." In that event you will have very successfully clutched promotion defeat from the jaws of victory!

Copying bad behavior

Many people are aggressive for the very simple reason that they see their own bosses apparently succeeding because of aggression. This may be a misconception. We are still, in the 1990s, only just beginning to appreciate the full value of "meritocracy," i.e., promotion according to merit rather than rank. Many people in the higher levels of our companies are still there because of hierarchy, who they know, and so on. In short, their aggression may not be the reason why they have been promoted, and some of them may even have been promoted higher were it not for their aggression. The role model is faulty but nonetheless often misperceived.

Because it works!

There is little point in denying that aggressive behavior can be very productive for the aggressor in some circumstances. This is of course an inducement to be aggressive or to continue aggressive behavior. However, in order to analyze this more fully, we should move on to the effects of aggression

The Effects of Aggression

The effects of aggression must be analyzed, as all behavioral types must be analyzed, for the immediate response they generate and the accumulated effects they cause.

The immediate responses generated

- You may feel less stressed because deadlines are met, crises are dealt with, and pressure is relieved. Aggression very quickly forces people to do what you want, removing those areas that create tension.
- Aggression can give a sense of control over others. Some of the more base instincts of humans include a liking for controlling other people.
- You can achieve a sense of pride if others praise your strength as a result of your aggressive stance.

These instant responses, in yourself and others, can make you feel good and increase the likelihood of your being seduced by aggressive behavior. However, you are instigating an accumulation of bad feeling against you, and within you.

Accumulated results of aggression

You become isolated by others

Aggressive statements tend to be exaggerated and polarized toward extremist views. Gradually this attitude isolates people from more rational-thinking individuals and increases the feeling of persecution, which in turn becomes a self-fulfilling prophecy, leaving the aggressor isolating himself.

Overly self-protective or paranoid

Sensing that they are being isolated by others, and blaming others because they cannot believe it relates to themselves, aggressive people become self-protective, "circling the wagons" around themselves. The wagons in this case refer to company rules, nonassertive subordinates, closed-door secrecy, and so on; anything that the aggressor can hide behind. When the aggressor does come out from inside the circle of wagons, it is usually in the manner of John Wayne in *True Grit*: the reins in his teeth and guns in both hands, aggressively sniping at all and anyone.

Tendency to blame others for bad relationships

The aggressive person finds that he does not sustain long-term relationships as he becomes tiresome and boring to others. Not believing that he is the cause of the problem, he will tend to blame other people for his bad relationships, giving excuses like "Oh, she only dislikes me because I am richer than her, got a promotion when she didn't, and so on."

People will not work for you

Aggressive people find that their aggression becomes self-fulfilling: they are not seen as the sort of people who can get people to work for them by enlightenment and people will only work for them when under threat. Consequently the aggressor has to maintain an aggressive threatening position in order to get people to work for him.

Worse, this leads to a cycle where subordinates believe that they have to be as aggressive as their boss so that they can have her job one day.

People resist you openly or "underground"

Assertive people, recognizing that they will not in the long term be treated in an aggressive manner, will openly resist aggressive people. If the aggressive individual happens to be their boss, then the resistance takes the form of working according to the rules and refusing to do otherwise quite reasonable overtime or additional duties; they also perform to a minimum standard of quality rather than their own higher potential. Nonassertive people tend to resist aggressive people "underground": spreading malicious rumors behind their backs, commenting on the aggressive person's mistakes or bad qualities, and ignoring his good qualities. This in turn becomes almost cyclical: the rumors that spread about an aggressive person are negative; these come back to the aggressive person, who feels under further threat and whose paranoia increases.

People seek revenge or conflict

Those people who feel most aggrieved by the actions of an aggressive person are almost waiting for their opportunity to get their own back or engage them in a conflict. If the opportunity does not arise, their own frustration builds up and when a better job opportunity arises they take it. If the opportunity does arise, then the disharmony and bad feeling will dominate the work environment for some time.

Feelings of guilt or shame

Aggressive people are not robots and are not inhuman. There are many times when they know that what they are doing is improper, though they are so entrenched in their behavior pattern that they are unable to break out of it. Furthermore, people whom they either are accustomed to listening to or are forced to listen to (their relationship partner, their own boss, trusted colleagues) will point out their deficiencies to them. This leads to a feeling of guilt or shame about the way they are treating others and about the fact that they are not respected by others. All studies indicate that people seek the approval of their colleagues, though aggressive people seem outwardly to reject it. Such feelings tend to lead to the onset of stress, characterized often by heavy drinking, failure to work effectively, psychosomatic illnesses such as backaches, headaches, and stomach problems, and so on.

There is a tendency to overcompensate with overfriendliness

One of the most unsettling aspects of relationships with aggressive people is that every now and again they try to mend their ways and be less aggressive. Although their attempts are in the main genuine, they do not understand the strength of assertion and tend to become overly friendly, even temporarily nonassertive. Unfortunately it is at this time that those with bottled up tension seek to make their move, attacking when the person is at his or her weakest and increasing the aggressor's feeling of persecution.

Why you become nonassertive

Fearing the response

Nonassertiveness is a habit and nonassertive people become accustomed to failing to stand up for their rights. Their everyday environment consists of responding in a way that avoids conflict, tries to gain the approval of others by being helpful and friendly, and so on. Such people, faced with the possibility of assertively standing up for their own rights, feel that they will be letting others down and that they will cease to be liked or will get into arguments they feel ill equipped to deal with.

Believing that assertiveness is aggressive

Nonassertive people, and particularly those whose early family life has been dominated by nonassertive role models, tend to see assertiveness as pushy or even aggressive. They equate these traits with unpleasant people. They also become angry when seeing people they regard as aggressive (actually assertive) getting what they want, getting better promotions, and so on. Unable to compete with such people, they reinforce in their own minds the belief that assertiveness is somehow an unpleasant trait that they do not wish to emulate. Their starting point is wrong and they are misreading the responses to their own behavior. The only way for them to understand that assertiveness is right for them is to act in an assertive manner and watch the results, which will be more positive than they are expecting.

Believing nonassertiveness to be politeness

Nonassertive people often believe that it is polite to comply with other people's requests and impolite to refuse their requests. They often believe that it is impolite to disagree with others and might, if they strongly disagree, merely remain silent rather than risk giving offense.

Believing nonassertiveness to be helpfulness

Nonassertive people often believe that by not putting forward their own beliefs, wishes, opinions, and so on, they are being helpful, in leaving the person they are speaking to with a wide number of options. The reverse is often true; the person they are speaking to would gladly meet their preferences if they expressed them, as quite often it is a matter of indifference to the other person as to which option is taken. If, for example, somebody asks you if you want caffeinated or decaffeinated coffee and you respond "Either would do," then you have not assisted the person in making a choice although it is probable that the person making the offer can make you one or the other coffee with ease. Your helpfulness has forced her to make a choice that may then turn out to be wrong; this is embarrassing if you admit later that you don't like the one she gave you.

By simply stating your preference, and you have been given permission to do this by the question in the first place, then not only do you stand up for your own rights, you also assist the person in making you comfortable and offering you what you want, which makes her feel good and considerate.

The difficulty with nonassertive people is that their inability to say no, combined with a belief that they are being helpful, often makes them extremely unreliable. For example, if you were to say to your junior secretary, "Would you please get this job done by the end of the day" and, no matter how many times you said that, he always said "yes" because he was unable to say "no," then you might well think that all the tasks you had given him would be done. However, at the end of the day you would discover that many of them had not been done as the time was not there, and you would then suddenly find yourself let down and possibly doing overtime to complete work you thought you had delegated. The junior secretary capable of saying "no" and giving a valid reason ("I already have a full quota of high-priority work that must be completed") leaves you with a clear understanding of the position and the time to find some other person to take on the task or to rearrange your own priorities in order to deal with it yourself. It is better to discover that at 10 o'clock in the morning than at 5:30 in the evening!

Feeling threatened

Just as people can become aggressive when feeling threatened, some become nonassertive. In the section on feeling threatened under aggression, we described the effect of cornering a tiger; similarly there are stories of animals that, if cornered, commit suicide: the ultimate nonassertiveness! In short, people respond differently and many people who feel threatened turn to nonassertiveness as a way of reducing the threat by placating others (being helpful, being polite, not being aggressive, and generally trying to be pleasing to others). This amounts to keeping your head down on the basis that, although you might not get promoted, on the other hand you might not get fired.

Failing to value yourself

We live in a world of self-fulfilling prophecies ("whether you believe you can, or whether you believe you can't, you are probably right"). For example, you and another secretary are going to your supervisor, both trying to get some word processor training days. The training can only be given to one of you. If you start by saying in your own mind "I know I won't get the training because Susan is "presenting her case so much better than I am," or "Susan always gets what she wants so I know I will lose the argument," then you will become defensive when putting across your request, whereas Susan is assertively explaining her requirement. Whenever your supervisor asks questions seeking information, you will interpret that as a sign of resistance and begin to withdraw your request, giving the subliminal message that you are not that interested anyway. Susan, on the other hand, will assertively enforce her rights and will give the impression of being enthusiastic and more likely to make use of the training than you will. Susan will get the training and this will reinforce your own belief that you are of less value than she is.

Failing to understand your own rights

Earlier we set out a sample of human and job rights. If you do not understand these, or accept these, then you cannot defend them.

The Effects of Nonassertiveness

Just as we saw with the effects of aggression, there have to be positive effects of nonassertion for it to be attractive enough to be self-maintaining. Again, the attractive effects are only immediate, with the longer-term accumulation being negative.

Immediate effects

Less stress

Conflict is avoided and tasks are done, usually with the thanks or even the praise of your colleagues or your boss. This serves to remove causes of stress that otherwise exist, particularly in times of work crisis

Feeling proud

The more you achieve, the more pride you feel. By taking on an impossible workload and achieving it, you feel increasingly proud. This becomes a drug and you seek more and more work and thereby more and more praise. Soon you will be the most praised person in the cardiac unit!

Indulgent self-pity

Nonassertive people have a victim mentality, enjoying the self-indulgence of "being treated harshly." To nonassertive people, this can feel quite rewarding until it tips over into self-pity in the longer term.

Avoiding guilt

By saying "yes" when we mean "no," taking on work we should not do, we avoid the feelings of guilt that might result from refusing other people's requests.

Accumulated effects

Increased self-pity

The fairly pleasant sensations of feeling sorry for yourself can become depressive if those sensations tip over into self-pity. Nonassertive people can acquire feelings of persecution and begin to recognize that their failures are damaging their career and their relationships.

Loss of others' respect of you

One of the longer-term effects of nonassertiveness is that other people lose their respect for you as they see you failing to stand up for your rights and seemingly being pressured by other people. The person who stands up to the bully, even if he or she gets a bloody nose, gains some respect; the person who runs away from the bully has at least displayed "discretion as the better part of valor"; but the victim who appears to like being bullied gains no respect at all.

Loss of self-worth

As you recognize that other people are being promoted above you, that you are failing to do work that you know you should be capable of, so you believe that you are "losing your touch" and you begin a cycle of believing yourself to be increasingly worthless.

Psychosomatic illnesses

In the longer term, nonassertive people often experience psychosomatic illnesses, such as headaches, backaches, and stomach disorders. There is some evidence to suggest that people can bring these illnesses on genuinely by their stresses, and further suggestions that these are psychological ways in which we avoid further conflict or give ourselves excuses for not being promoted ("I couldn't do the job anyway because I haven't been well for a while . . .").

Conflict caused by overcommitment, e.g., home versus office

Nonassertive people often take on more work than they can complete and end up having to do overtime to meet the commitments they have made. In turn, this leads to others expecting them to do overtime and becomes a cycle so unbreakable that when they need to leave work on time the others feel that they are somehow letting the group down. Alternatively, some people are able to work anywhere there is a calculator or a desk, and they will often stuff a briefcase at the end of the day, take it home, and work in the evening. Either way, the office is beginning to impinge on home life. This of course creates conflicts in the home, which add to stress and a feeling of a threatened lifestyle, increasing the possibility of further nonassertive behavior in order to avoid further conflict.

The end result of nonassertion is that the person who is setting out trying to be liked by everyone ends up becoming irritating and failing to gain the respect of his colleagues. By constantly saying "yes" when he should have said "no" and taking on more work than he can deal with, he will at some point let people down and become a source of irritation in this way. Eventually nonassertive people start to become avoided by those who prefer straightforwardness.

Dealing Assertively with Nonassertion

As we have already seen, nonassertive people are difficult to deal with. They make promises they cannot keep, they let you down, and they do not make clear what they want or need. It is in your interests not only to deal assertively with them but to encourage them to be assertive for everyone's benefit.

Take the following situation. You have asked Susan to prepare a job roster for your department. She replies nonassertively, "Well, all right then, but I'm not very good at organizing that sort of thing. I messed up the last one." She is putting herself down, preparing the ground for a failure that she will make come true if you let her and trying to get out of the task. Furthermore, she is trying to transfer responsibility for the failure to you, on the grounds that you asked someone who was not the right person for the job.

Your reply should be (on the basis that you believe she was the right person for the job): "You may have had problems with the last one, but I disagree that you are not good at the task generally. Let's sit down together and see if we can work out what the problems were and plan a way of overcoming them." This avoids mollycoddling or being patronizing and encourages the person to work out the task for herself but with your support.

Take a second situation. You ask Peter to get the outstanding accounts payable report to you for typing by the end of the week, having worked out that this is a reasonable request and one that will enable you to meet deadlines you have committed yourself to. Peter says, "I'm really swamped with work at the moment, I don't think I've got time. However, I'll try and fit it in." What Peter is doing is leaving the door open for letting you down and then saying, "I told you so." In short, and as Susan did above, he is transferring responsibility for the failure to you and apologizing for that failure in advance. Your goal is to force him to be assertive, which will be good for him and good for you.

You start by responding, "This is an important task that has to be done to a deadline. Let me look at your work schedule with you and we will see if we can work out a reprioritization between us." Nonassertive people will almost inevitably have a weak and incorrect schedule of priorities, usually based on what they would like to do rather than what needs doing. You will almost certainly be able to reorganize Peter's work program to his advantage. Having done this, you must concur with him on a commitment that he must make (i.e., not imposed by you). You can then say to Peter, "It looks to me as if you could probably have this done by 3 o'clock on Friday, which will give me time to do what I have to do with it. Do you agree?"

Peter may vacillate a bit but in the end you must get him to say the equivalent of, or agree to the equivalent of, "Yes, I will have this done and delivered to you by 3 o'clock on Friday." Now he has made a firm specific commitment. You have not imposed the deadline on him, he has agreed to it with you. It is therefore his deadline and his failure alone if he does not meet it. Having failed to transfer the responsibility to you, it now weighs more heavily on him. Having made the commitment to do the task he has implicitly agreed that he is able to do it, and you cannot be blamed for "picking the wrong person." He should strive harder to achieve the commitment, or be open to constructive criticism if he fails to do so (and be sure that you constructively challenge any failure of commitments).

Apart from the fact that you increase the probability of getting the job done properly and on time, you increase the probability that Peter will feel good about the job as he will feel it is within his control and that he can achieve it. Be sure to give appropriate praise openly and genuinely if he does achieve his commitment.

This will make him seek further achievements and you will have put him on the path toward assertiveness.

Remember the golden rule that assertiveness is the easiest behavior to deal with and that part of learning assertiveness is learning how to make others assertive too.

Dealing with Aggression in Others

The principle in handling aggression from others is to remain assertive yourself. A secondary effect is that in the long term you will display benefits of assertiveness and encourage aggressive people to see how powerful assertion can be, it is hoped; just as you can make nonassertive people assertive, you can make aggressive people assertive. The effect is the same: they become easier to deal with in ways that are both positive and respecting of themselves.

Take the following situation. You are questioning Katie about a work-related problem. She is continually late for work. Throughout this dialogue, Katie remains persistently aggressive.

Your dialogue is a progressive one through the various levels of assertiveness. You will probably start with a statement of basic assertiveness. "You have been late by more than half an hour eight times this month. I do not want you to be late again. By the end of next month, I want to see that you have not been late any day in that month." This is basic assertion: You have made a straightforward statement of the situation and your requirements, giving specific measurable goals to be achieved.

In this scenario, Katie is persistently aggressive and in this instance responds, "I do my best. I'll get here when I can."

You move to questioning assertion. "That is not good enough. I have explained what I want in the future. Can you tell me why this creates a problem for you?" You have responded intelligently to her comment; if she claims she is doing her best and if that is not acceptable then you are asking her what problem she is having that prevents her from getting to work on time. (In certain situations you might have started this dialogue with questioning assertion; in the example, we have assumed that there is no doubt of her lateness. If there is any doubt, e.g., you received the information thirdhand, then it would be sensible to start with questioning assertion to determine whether or not the information you had is correct.)

Katie again responds aggressively: "It's none of your damned business what the problem is."

Having been given no tangible description of the problem, you are not likely to move on to empathetic assertion, as there is no common ground on which to have empathy. You might say something like, "I can see that this is a real problem for you. However, I need you to be here on time. By taking the job you have committed yourself to that, and I must insist that you are." If you are given a specific problem, then you might have grounds for empathy but this would not weaken your resolve.

Whatever Katie's response, which we are assuming is persistently aggressive, you will have to move on to negative feelings assertion. In this instance, it is likely to take two forms: one relating to the undesirable effect Katie's lateness is having and the second relating to the undesirable effect her attitude in this conversation is having. "Your failure to get here on time means that your work is partly being done by others and this department is falling behind its deadlines. This is disruptive to me. In the future, I want you to keep to the terms of the contract to which you are committed and be here on time. Furthermore, your aggressiveness right now is making this conversation difficult, but it is a conversation we must have as your lateness is a behavior that must change." You are beginning to exhibit another requirement of assertiveness: the "stuck record" technique, reinforcing and not withdrawing your standpoint.

Katie, at this point, assuming she continues aggressively, either argues her point or, quite possibly, says little other then "Get lost!" (or something less polite).

It is highly likely that in going through these levels you will at some point force Katie into a constructive dialogue, but in instances where failure is persistent, you have no option but to go to outcome assertiveness. "If you are late again, then I have no alternative but to give you a written warning. Furthermore I must report it to your boss. (Assuming that there is a boss over your department to which you report.) Your being on time in the future will avoid this. I would prefer not to have to deal with it this way."

You have said the last thing that needs to be said on your part. If Katie responds constructively, then you get her to make a commitment assertively (as we did with Peter in dealing with nonassertiveness), but if she continues to ignore you there is nothing further for you to do than to carry out precisely what you have committed yourself to do.

There are alternative scenarios to be considered.

Alternative scenario 1

Katie throughout the entire conversation never says a word but stands aggressively, glaring at you as you try to reason. Do not waste your time going all the way through the levels of assertiveness. After using discrepancy assertiveness, point out to Katie that if she is not prepared to bring down her aggressive barriers you will end this discussion now, but that you will return to it at a later time. Specify the exact time at which she is to come to you to continue the discussion. It is highly likely that faced with that Katie will decide to get into dialogue with you then and there, in which case you carry on as above. Should she take up your offer and come back at a specified time, you will have to go through all the levels, possibly with no particular response from Katie, but to do it fairly swiftly and to make your outcome assertiveness very clear.

Alternative scenario 2

You persuade Katie to make a commitment to be on time in the future. Remember that she may have made that commitment simply to get you off her back. She may have no intention to meet the commitment she has made. First, you should still agree on a specific deadline for reviewing the current position. You should say, "I appreciate your making that commitment. I would like to arrange now for us to get together at the end of next month (specify a time and date) so that we can look over your attendance record then." If when you do this she has met her commitment, remember to give open, genuine, praise. If she has not met her commitment, then you should use discrepancy assertiveness. "Last month we agreed that you would arrive at work on time every day. I see from the record that you have not done so. I would like you to explain why not so that we can look at the situation and make sure that next month this will not happen again." The further levels of assertiveness are open to you in this situation.

Alternative scenario 3

At any point during the levels of the dialogue, Katie might accept the position you are putting forward and make a commitment. Make sure that the commitment is specific and to a deadline, and agree a time to review it as before. Do not, of course, move on to other levels of assertiveness unnecessarily.

Recognizing Behavior Styles

There are certain verbal and nonverbal signals that indicate an aggressive stance, nonassertive behavior, or an assertive character. It is important that you are able to recognize these, not just in yourself but in others. Once you know you are dealing with a nonassertive or aggressive person, you can adapt your own game plan accordingly. The best game plan in assertiveness is to set up situations where the person you are dealing with becomes assertive; then she becomes easier to deal with. So assertiveness is not just about becoming assertive yourself but also about encouraging others to do so too. The starting point is to recognize where they are coming from.

Some analyzes of communication have indicated that as much as 80 percent of the meaning of our presentations to others is transmitted through eye contact and body language. Certainly it is important to realize that even assertive language delivered in an aggressive or nonassertive way creates an uncomfortable inconsistency that is very offputting to the person we are speaking to. There follow summaries of the nonverbal behaviors of aggression, nonassertiveness and assertiveness.

Aggression

Verbal signals of aggression

Excessively egocentric statements

These might be: "I need this done," or "My opinion is that." These statements indicate that the person is thinking of himself more than others and values himself above others. Do note that the verbal signals of assertion also contain ego-centered statements, but of a different nature (the person is taking responsibility for himself). Sometimes the words alone do not convey the significance: the analysis has to be combined with a tone of voice and a body posture. These are covered below under nonverbal signals.

Put-downs

Aggressive people believe that their own viewpoints should dominate and will use phrases like "I don't care what you think," or "who cares what your opinion is?"

Threats or implied threats

Questions that carry an implication of threat, such as "Why haven't you completed that report typing yet?" (again coupled with a threatening tone of voice), seek to steal the initiative from other people and put them on the defensive from the outset.

Disguised orders

When your supervisor says, "We should do it this way, shouldn't we?," he may well be instructing you to do it that way and not really asking a question at all. It is typical of the verbal signals of aggression that words that should be used in a genuinely questioning way or in a manner that seeks to build bridges are in fact commands designed to get the aggressor's own way over and above the rights of others.

People expressing their opinions as facts

It is often difficult to tell the difference between opinion and a fact, particularly when it comes out of the mouth of an aggressive person. As we have often said, the one clue that is offered is that when an aggressive person thumps the table, goes red in the face, and shouts "And that's a fact!," she is almost certainly expressing her opinion.

People singing their own praises

Aggressive people make the most of their successes and even occasionally rewrite history to make more of them than there is. Generally a statement like "My department always meets its budgetary deadlines" is often a form of attack that comes from insecurity (e.g., knowing that the department is falling down in other ways).

Implied blame

Implied blame follows from boasting and can be used to turn the tables on others, forcing them on the defensive. For example, there may be an implied and unspoken ending in the statement "My department always meets its budgetary deadlines (unlike your department)." The part of the sentence in parentheses is unspoken but implied.

Hiding behind the rule book

Aggressive people often make statements that criticize others on the basis of their not obeying some unwritten intangible rule book, e.g., "You ought to do this," or "You had better do such and such." Such statements impose the aggressor's moral or other standards on others, without giving the other person the chance to express her own beliefs or opinions.

Overgeneralizations

Aggressive people always feel that the rest of the world is out of step with them, and will make overgeneralized statements, such as "It's all the fault of the youth of today." Such statements are of course meaningless, and are often presented so aggressively that they force the people listening to them to agree, even if they then comment unfavorably on the aggressor behind his back.

Blatantly rude assumptions

Aggressive people may ask if something is completed by saying, "I suppose you haven't finished this yet?" Rather like an overgeneralization, such blatantly rude assumptions make it difficult for the person being challenged to defend herself if the task has not been completed. There may be a very good reason why the task has not been completed, but the blatantly rude assumption makes even the most valid reason sound like an excuse. (We will come to dealing with aggression below, but in this instance it is worth noting that to respond to the assumption is to fall into the trap; the appropriate response is to challenge the assumption, e.g., "On what basis do you assume that . . .?")

Nonverbal behavior of aggression

Verbal delivery
- Fast and fluent, without hesitation.
- Rude and abrupt, often with sentence fragments delivering unjustified commands.
- Emphasizing words that put down others.
- Harsh (and "no nonsense").
- Cold and unfeeling.
- Often sarcastic.
- Loud.
- The pitch of the voice may rise at the end of sentences (in extreme cases almost to hysteria—look at the speeches of Adolf Hitler).

Expression and use of facial features
- Smiles at victories (a smile reminiscent of a cat left in a room alone with a goldfish).
- Tries to frighten others by extreme expressions.
- Raising eyebrows in an attempt to intimidate by pretending astonishment at what he is being told.
- Eye contact fixed directly eye-to-eye with no letup (very uncomfortable).

Body language
- Fingers thrusting accusingly toward people.
- Banging tables, chair arms, hand into hand.
- Leaning into the person she is speaking to.
- Physically dominating others by moving improperly close to them (works best for taller or bulkier people).

- Arms crossed high on the chest ("Approach me if you dare").
- Makes impatience clear by openly and rudely tapping fingers, striding around the room, speaking loudly while looking out of windows, and so on.

Nonassertiveness

Verbal signals of nonassertiveness

The main message of the verbal signals of nonassertiveness is to transfer responsibility from the nonassertive person to someone else in order that, if anything goes wrong, creates problems, or annoys others, it can be blamed on another person, the company, or the person being addressed.

Overapologetic

An example might be, "I'm awfully terribly sorry but . . ." Politeness demands appropriate apologies when we have let people down, but elaborate apologies become irritating and uncomfortable for the person being apologized to.

Transferring responsibility by seeking permission

Phrases such as "I'm sure you don't mind, do you?" might be used. This is a clear sign that people are afraid to take responsibility and they are transferring their responsibility to others implying that if something goes wrong, the blame belongs to the other person.

Long and tortuous sentences

Nonassertive people are never certain of their ground, always feeling that they have overlooked some important fact, that they will be challenged on some aspect of their opinion, and so on. They use long tortuous sentences in a combination of insecurity (keeping talking so the other person hasn't got a chance to challenge them), "blinding them with science" (trying to sound well educated and impressive to head off challenges), and "searching for signals" (keeping talking so that they can monitor the reaction of the person they are talking to see if what they are saying is favorable to him or her). When people are on certain ground and feel assertive, they are able to express themselves in short simple sentences that demonstrate their control of the situation.

Avoiding the subject

Quite often nonassertive people will skirt around the subject that needs to be discussed, sometimes avoiding it completely but hinting at it in the hope that the person they are speaking to will raise it. This is another method by which nonassertive people transfer the responsibility for the subject to others.

Padding

Along with long and tortuous sentences and attempting to avoid the subject entirely, nonassertive people fill in their thinking time during speech by constantly introducing meaningless padding, such as "uhm," "ahh," "well," "like," and "know what I mean?"

Overcasual

Sometimes nonassertive people will attempt to pass off an obviously important point as if it was of no consequence. For example, they might "drop in" to their supervisor's or boss's office and say, "I just happen to be passing so I thought I'd mention that I'd like a salary increase." The reason for attempting to be overcasual is twofold: first, it seeks to justify the reason for making a request (i.e., I was here anyway so I thought I ought to mention it now); second, it presents the image of the request not being very important or serious, so that, if refused, the person can try to dismiss it lightly (in his own mind) and pretend to himself that it wasn't very important anyway.

These are, of course, completely false reasonings. The request for a salary increase is a serious one and should not need further justification. It is not credible for anyone to assume that you would ask for a salary increase on the spur of the moment just because you happen to be passing a door. Such an approach looks weak and nonassertive and will encourage a refusal; in fact, it almost literally asks for one.

The puppeteer

Nonassertive people will transfer responsibility by assigning control of the situation to someone else. For example, if a nonassertive supervisor has to give work to her subordinate or criticize the work of the subordinate she might start by saying, "I have been told I have to do this . . ." Or she will hide behind the rule book (written or unwritten), and even go so far as to combine being overapologetic with blaming others, using phrases such as "I personally don't think you've done anything wrong, but I have been asked to tell you that . . ."

Self-devaluation

Nonassertive people, not knowing or standing up for their rights, often combine the acceptance of requests they cannot deal with, with excuses that preempt their inevitable failure. They may be asked to do a particular job and they will say, "I need more resources but don't worry about me, I'll struggle on." This gives them the short-term pleasure of trying to win against all the odds and the long-term dissatisfaction of constantly losing against all the odds, which seem to be piled up on them by other people. They are of course setting up reasons why they are going to fail and on the basis of self-fulfilling prophecy increasing the probability that they will.

Put-downs

Nonassertive people often try to get out of work that they don't want to do or even perhaps genuinely feel they are unable to do, using phrases such as "I'm terrible at this," or "I've never been very good at . . ." Rather like self-devaluation, this sets up a situation where the person has a ready-made excuse, delivered ahead of failure, for self-fulfilling failure. The phrases are also used to try to gain the approval of others by encouraging them along ("Oh no, you are really very good at . . ."). Again, they end up doing the task "against all the odds" and failing because of "unreasonable requests being made of me."

Saying nothing

Quite often the most nonassertive response to being spoken to is to say nothing in response, accepting whatever improper (or proper) criticism is made. Nonassertive people might also say nothing when they should be raising an issue with someone else. The quiet mouse in the corner of the room, not upsetting anyone, not getting under anyone's feet, and so on, not only sends out vague and uncertain signals to other people but is probably bottling up a great many long-term negative effects of nonassertiveness.

Nonverbal behavior of nonassertiveness

Verbal delivery

- Pauses created with uhms, ahhs, coughing.
- Inconsistent speed of delivery of speech, sometimes cautious, sometimes hurried (as if to get it over with).
- Unfinished sentences.
- Uncertain, faltering.
- Inappropriately higher pitch than usual.
- Overfriendliness.
- Featureless, dull (trying to hide behind the potted plants!).

Expression and use of facial features

- Smiling falsely when being angry or receiving criticism.
- Eyes wide and eyebrows raised as if in constant amazement or anticipation of criticism.
- Inappropriate expressions (such as smiling while criticizing).
- Eyes darting around the room; unable to make sustained eye contact.
- Looking at the floor or the person's feet. (The most astonishing example we saw of this became so irritating to the person being spoken to that he actually addressed it verbally. We were watching a conversation where the person speaking was not only looking down at her own feet but at 90 degrees to the person she was speaking to, who was off to her left. Eventually the person she was speaking to was forced to make the comment, "You do realize I'm standing over here, don't you.")

Body language

- Inconsistent body language, such as asking a question that would seem to demand a "yes" while shaking his own head as if to invite a "no."
- Anguished hand-wringing.
- Retreating toward the door.
- Cowering (and general attempts to diminish the overall size of her body to imply "I'm only a small mouse, please don't hurt me").
- When talking, hiding his mouth behind his hand as if to imply that the words being spoken are not that significant.

- Displacement activities (fidgeting). When we have nervous energy to dispel, we tend to do so by physically fidgeting with ourselves or other objects, at great discomfort to others.
- Arms crossed low (seeking protection from attack).

Assertiveness

The verbal signals of assertiveness

Assertive people do not transfer responsibility to others but take responsibility for themselves. They do not threaten or attack others, but use phrases that seek to build bridges, look into preferences that can be used to build constructive compromises, and give criticism where necessary, with a view toward offering help rather than blame.

Self-responsible statements

Rather like aggressive people, assertive people use statements with many "I's in them, but in a context that takes responsibility as opposed to transferring it elsewhere; for example, "I would like to implement this change" (as opposed to "The usual rules are to . . ."). Self-responsible statements differ from ego-centered statements in the body language and eye contact that go with them.

Clear, concise, simple statements

Rather than using the long, tortuous sentences of nonassertion or the blaming and boasting of aggression, assertive people make clear statements that are direct and to the point and leave others in no doubt of the position they are taking; for example, "I would like to implement this new filing system from the beginning of the next quarter." Such a statement takes responsibility for the decision, makes clear to others what is required and when, and does not prevent people from commenting on or questioning the statement.

Open attitudes

When there is genuine doubt or uncertainty, the assertive person uses language that seeks constructive solution and offers cooperation rather than demands, e.g., "Can we work together to find a solution to this?"

Open questioning

Rather using the question as an implied or hidden command (like the aggressive person) or as a means of transferring responsibility to others (like the nonassertive person), the assertive person uses questioning that genuinely and openly is ready for feedback, e.g., "Do you think it would be effective to try this?" Such phrases invite a response, even a negative one, on which alternatives can be built in discussion.

Recognition of the difference between fact and opinion

Unlike the aggressor, who disguises her opinions as if they were facts that seem to be unchallengeable, or the nonassertive person, who rarely offers his own opinion anyway, the assertive person makes a clear distinction between fact and opinion. For example, there may be a new word processor system installed in the computers, and the assertive person may say of it, "I like this system." This is a clear statement of his opinion rather than an attempt to disguise it as a fact, which would force people to go along with it. Such attempts might be "This is a good system," or "This is the best system on the market," which sound like definitive and unarguable statements.

Constructive criticism

Rather than using criticism that blames others or inviting criticism from others, assertive people give criticism in a way that deals with situations rather than personalities and allows for agreement to future changes. For example, an assertive person would say "Sandra, I have noticed that your typing has contained a lot of errors lately" (which addresses the problem), rather then "Sandra, you have become a bad typist lately" (which blames Sandra personally and does not specify the reason for the comment). The question of giving constructive criticism is covered below.

Nonverbal behavior of assertiveness

Verbal delivery
- Demonstrates good command of language.
- Few pauses.
- Emphasizes important words, not blaming words or responsibility transferring words.
- Controlled speed of delivery.
- Clear, firm.
- Consistent tone and pitch (not shouting or whining).
- Warm.
- Sincere.

Expression and use of facial features
- Appropriate smiles.
- Appropriate expressions when angry or displeased (frowning).
- Open expression when listening to others.
- Generally relaxed face.
- Maintained eye contact but with appropriate glances aside or movements around the face to prevent staring down. Contact maintained in the face triangle (i.e., eye contact is not always directly to the eyes but to the area of the face covered by a triangle bordered by the eyes and the nose down to the top of the lip).

Body language
- Arms not crossed, thereby inviting openness.
- Relaxed and friendly gestures.
- Upright posture.
- Head level, not looking up or looking down.
- Leaning forward for emphasis, not for attack.

Becoming Assertive

We have already said that we approach the question of becoming assertive by interrupting the belief–behavior cycle by changing behavior rather than beliefs. These behavioral changes must be consistent if they are to become natural. It is important to recognize that you cannot address the question of becoming assertive at work if you do not also address the question of becoming assertive elsewhere in your life. It is obvious in any case that if you accept that there are benefits to assertiveness, you would want those benefits to be with you 24 hours a day rather than just for the eight or so hours you are at work. However, the changes that you will make can cause conflict to your spouse or partner.

Why should this be?

In all relationships, whether at work, at home or in day-to-day life, we negotiate rules and conditions for interaction. It is aggressive and rude to change those rules unilaterally, because they have been negotiated with others; we can only change them in a way that recognizes the negotiation and allows for it.

To take an example from home life, let us suppose that a woman has for all the years of her marriage cooked all her husband's meals. She might come to the conclusion that a fairer balance of duties around the house is for her husband to cook some meals himself, or to at least join her in the kitchen when she is cooking. If she addresses this question one evening by just announcing that there will be no further meals until her husband changes his ways, then she is being unfairly aggressive. From her husband's point of view, he has done nothing different, apparently nothing to cause offense; yet suddenly he is in effect being punished. The proper way to address this situation is to discuss how it arose and what changes are sought and to negotiate—perhaps over a meal—a new set of rules. It is important to recognize that people fill up their time as available and that, if he is suddenly faced with having to cook a meal, the husband will have to give up something he is doing (even if it is something that the wife regards as wasting time, such as watching TV or playing golf). Recognition of this on the wife's part shows that, while sticking up for her own rights, she is also recognizing the rights of her husband.

The same rules apply in work when you are dissatisfied with the work you are being asked to do. You must recognize that if you are already doing it, you have implicitly agreed that it was appropriate, at least at some time. In order to make changes you have to enter into negotiation, which recognizes that if you are not going to do it someone else will have to and that her responsibilities and workload will have to be taken into account. We mentioned earlier the case of the woman who had discovered that her boss regarded it as part of her duties to peel his oranges. As we said there, she could not simply refuse on one occasion but would have to accept the fact that by doing it she had implicitly negotiated agreement to that situation, and that she would have to renegotiate a new position from a standpoint that recognized that he could rightly regard her peeling his oranges as normal until such time as the rules were changed between them.

Reprogram Yourself

Some of the practical changes that you will make can be made at home or in the office. It is useful, however, to consider why changes are necessary and how you got to be the person you currently are.

Who created you?

The "you" that is now reading this book is the "you" of today. It is not the "you" of yesterday, nor is it the "you" of tomorrow, both of whom will be subtly different. Today you were coming home on the train and someone dropped her bag, you picked it up for her and she thanked you. The person opposite said how nice it was to see considerate people, which made you feel good. Suddenly commuting was not so unpleasant after all; in fact the whole world looked a bit rosier. Or perhaps today was not a good day. You were coming home on the train and you were nearly knocked off your feet by an extremely rude individual, who marched on ignoring your protestations. Suddenly commuting was an awful chore; the world looked gray.

Of course, these are temporary effects and we recognize them as such. But they also add to our sum total of experience and knowledge about the world and they make tiny permanent changes to our view of the world around us.

But what about the major events: that unforgettable four-week holiday touring the world, or the tragic and painful death of a loved one. In an extreme case, if we took a person here and now and analyzed what made him the character and personality that he is, and if tonight his infant child died suddenly, he would never again be that person. The person who would go on into the future from that incident could permanently be a different person. In many cases he would be a wounded person, in some cases perhaps even an enhanced person—some people have an enviable ability to find the positive in any situation—but certainly a different person.

So how did you get to be the person you are? You were created by your parents in far more than the biological sense: they were the first dominant influence on your life. For many years they dictated whether you got what you wanted or needed, or whether you did not, they dictated their view of what was right and what was wrong and they influenced your own decisions in that way. They were your first role models.

In addition to your parents, there were your friends, your teachers, in many cases your spiritual leaders, other relatives in your family, classmates who may or may not have been your friends, members of clubs and societies you joined, your neighbors, and people at large in society. On a more remote level, there are the influences of government decisions, what you read in the media, writers whose works you have read or directors whose films and programs you have watched, advertisers, and so on. All of these people had a view of the world and they imposed it on you, in most cases because they genuinely believed it was for your good; and it might have been.

Some of the influences may have been very unsubtle: indoctrination, rewards and punishment, censoring of data, suppression of argument, and so on. Some may have been more subtle: praise when you conform to standards, acceptance when you act and behave as expected or wanted; the peer pressure of your friends to dress as they do, listen to the records they listen to, see the films they see, and act as they act.

But there is one person missing from this list of influences on your life. You.

Many people go through life without ever consciously taking control of themselves. They believe they are making decisions, of course; but at best these are often decisions based on a choice presented by others. Take, for example, the influence of religion. Why are there so many Christians in the British Isles and so many Hindus in India? The particular clusterings of all religious groups around the world are based on the fact that people are born into those religions, either in the family or in the community. People are Christian, Hindu, or other religions because they are told to be: it is the way they are brought up.

Take Control of Your Own Life

There are practical ways in which you can begin to become an influence in the you that will go forward from this day. And if you are serious about developing assertiveness, then you should begin to practice these from now.

Review your beliefs

Right now write out a list of 20 things you strongly believe in; for example, "I believe it is wrong to murder," "I believe in God," "I believe in being faithful in marriage," "I believe it is acceptable to kill animals." Each month make it your rule to review one of these beliefs in depth. Keep a notepad by your bed and by your side at all times. Jot down your answers to questions like:

- When was I first conscious of this belief?
- Who do I think is most influential in guiding me to this belief?
- What would be the consequences in my life if I found I no longer believed this?
- Why do I believe this? (For example, for the belief "I believe it is right to be faithful in marriage," do you believe this because it is morally correct, because it is expected of you, or because you fear the consequences of an alternative course of action?)

You will think of many more questions; answer them. Spend your month analyzing your beliefs until you know all the influences that have created them and all the reasons why you hold them to be true (conviction, guilt, fear, peer pressure).

Then challenge every one of your statements. Ask yourself why you fear peer pressure and what the consequences of ignoring it will be. Make sure from this point onward that you hold the beliefs you hold because no other reality would make sense to you. In many cases, you will find that you will still hold the belief you started with. This is partly because it is difficult to shake off a lifetime of influence, but partly because you will have gone through filtering processes through your life but will have rejected the more extreme alternatives in your mind. From now onward, however, you can go forward knowing that you believe what you believe because you have thought it out, you have understood the influences, and you have made the appropriate decisions. The very least you can achieve is that, by recognizing that your beliefs are shaped by others and you cannot change them, you will have recognized the influence of others. In years to come, you will find that you have strengthened yourself because of this, but the more quickly you can begin the changes the better.

Remember to review negative beliefs too; for example, "I believe life has to be a struggle," "I believe money is the cause of evil in the world," "I believe you have to suffer before you can be happy," "I believe you give up your freedom when you marry."

Make this monthly review of your beliefs something you do indefinitely.

Make commitments to yourself

Many people feel that they have no control in their lives because they cannot even accomplish small tasks: rearranging the filing system (which you have meant to do for some time), clearing out that kitchen drawer, tidying up the garden shed, and so on. The reason these things don't get done is that we fail to plan to do them and there is often limited, if any, incentive to do them other than the fact that we know we ought to.

Buy a pack of small index cards, a box of pushpins, and a large bulletin board. Put the bulletin board up somewhere prominently in your house, in either the kitchen or the hall. On your cards, write out commitments to things you will do. These must be practical not conceptual. For example, do not put "I will become a better person tomorrow," because such statements are too intangible and success or achievement cannot be measured. Put statements like the following:

- I will tidy up the kitchen drawer by 9 o'clock this Friday evening.
- I will begin reorganizing my filing system on Monday and I will complete the reorganization by Friday in three weeks' time.
- I will go to the bookstore and order the book I have been halfheartedly hoping to find first thing on Monday morning.
- I will telephone a plumber to get the dripping faucet fixed by no later than Wednesday this week (it is also my goal that the faucet should be fixed by the end of Friday in the following week).
- I will present a plan to my boss to have the photocopier moved into another agreed location by the end of the following week (see Solutions not problems, following).

Over time you will be able to fill out hundreds of such cards. Every time you recognize that a task needs doing, complete a card for it. Review your cards frequently and make sure that your commitments to yourself are made. Not only will you get done a lot of what you have been meaning to get done, you will also recognize that you have achieved it through your own determined planning. You will feel very much more in control of your life and the world around you.

It is important to write down not just the task you are going to do but also the time by which you are going to do it, as otherwise there is a temptation to live in a world where things will always get done sometime.

There is a third component that needs to be mentioned. You should promise yourself and give yourself rewards for these tasks. The rewards must be realistic and matched to the task. For example, you can hardly promise yourself a three-week Mediterranean cruise for cleaning out the kitchen drawer! You might consider rewards such as agreeing with your partner that at the completion of a certain task you are entitled to a glass of wine and half an hour of uninterrupted peace listening to your favorite music or watching your favorite TV program, or being pampered with breakfast in bed on Sunday morning (remember that your partner will also have a set of commitments and rewards and you should play your part in helping him or her by taking part in his or her rewards—fair is fair!). You may have to take similar private rewards for your achievements at work unless yours is an enlightened firm that motivates by using these reward systems. You might consider, when supervising others, that you should introduce some system like this in your department if you can get your boss to agree to it.

Never shirk on rewards you have promised yourself. If you have promised yourself a night out at the theater for a particular task and you complete the task, do not then say, "But I can't really afford it, perhaps I will do it some other time." Imagine that you were to promise your staff a reward for doing some task, such as a day off or some overtime money, and then when they had completed the task you told them, "Well, I'm sorry but we can't afford it right now, perhaps some other time." You would not get that member of staff to work for you on that basis again. Your relationship with your own subconscious is no different. If you fail to give yourself your rewards, you will be reluctant to undertake your own tasks in the future, as your subconscious will know it has been cheated. You must bathe in the "feel good" factor. The rewards will be a tangible round of applause for your success and will encourage you further.

Some assertiveness courses and books recommend this card system for statements of reprogramming yourself such as "I can . . .," "I will . . .," "I am . . .," and so on. These can be effective for some people but we find much greater success and much more lasting success from measurable practical achievements that show the control you are having over your own life, replacing "I will . . ." with "I will do . . ."

Finally, the trophy system is a further reinforcement. When you have completed your task on your card, pin it to the bulletin board with pushpins. Keep them up there over time, new cards covering old ones. They can become a conversation piece and you will feel good about the interest and admiration they create. The blank bulletin board on the wall is also a useful incentive at the beginning, as people will ask you: "What's that for?" Obviously, if you can have a similar bulletin board at work for your workplace commitments, this is all the better; encourage it in all your staff and colleagues.

Solutions, not problems

In the work environment particularly, we have to recognize that the commitments we set and the achievement of those is not always totally at our discretion. We are often subject to the agreement of our boss or others. It is worth recognizing this when setting the commitment in order not to make it impractical. For example, if you want to change a company procedure that affects you, it may be impractical to make that a commitment if achieving it is dependent on others and on forces outside your control. But you can make as your commitment that you will prepare your presentation by a certain date and deliver it then. (You can make the change a goal rather than a commitment, because a goal is something you can work to over a long period of time in practical stages.)

More importantly, it is worth increasing your chances of success when your commitments (or even your goals) are dependent on the agreement or cooperation of others. The most successful rule here is "offer solutions, not problems." Margaret Thatcher always said of Lord Young that what pleased her most was that he brought her solutions rather than problems. You should adopt similar principles.

In the preceding text, we considered the question of your making a commitment to get a photocopier moved from one location to another. Let us look at that in more detail in a way that offers the greatest probability of success.

The situation is that you have a photocopier in your office or next to your workstation. It is noisy and intrusive. Furthermore, people using the photocopier tend to use your desk as a place to put papers while they are copying. Because you are there, they think that you are the photocopy person and often ask you to do them a favor.

What not to do

Do not repeatedly go to your boss and say, "Please can you get the photocopier moved?" By doing this you will be giving her a problem. She will have to work out a solution and organize its implementation. It is far more likely that she will say to you, "I'll do it just as soon as I can get around to it," and you will wait forever. In the interim, between now and forever, you will keep annoying your boss by repeating your request and you will increase your own frustration as the situation continues.

What you should do

Create the solution. First, locate alternative sites for the photocopier. Talk to the people who are around those sites and negotiate with them the best position. There may be a more out-of-the-way place that can be set up for the photocopier or a more convenient location, possibly even more helpful to someone else. Make sure that there is a power supply at that location, and cupboards for appropriate stationery or a place for them to be moved to. Perhaps try to find an old table or desk that can be set up nearby so that people will have a place to put their papers if necessary. Then take the package to your boss and say, "The photocopier is causing me difficulties because . . . I have worked out a plan for its relocation at this site" (and explain the facilities you have been able to set up). "I have spoken to the people in that area and they are happy for it to be located there. I would therefore like to move the photocopier, or arrange for its removal, first thing tomorrow morning unless you have any objections to this. If you do have objections, perhaps you could explain them to me." Ninety-nine times out of a hundred, your boss will accept your proposals for two simple reasons:

1. There are probably few reasonable objections to be raised if you have done your groundwork well.
2. If he or she complies with your request, the problem completely goes away and he or she will not have to think about it again. This is too tempting for most bosses!

Apply the principle of offering solutions and not problems to as many of your requests as possible and you will transform the world around you more quickly than using almost any other approach.

Giving Praise

Unfortunately most people work in an environment where praise is rare but criticism is common. This is reflected even in the way computer reports are set up for business, i.e., exception reporting. There is an assumption that compliance with requirements is "normal," and comment is usual only on things that are exceptional (usually cause for concern). We tend to act that way toward people too. We believe that they should give us an acceptable standard of work and comment only when they fail to do so. It would be very constructive to make giving praise when people do well at least on a par with giving criticism when they do not.

Because we rarely give praise in business, it is usually done badly. One attempt we heard was: "You ran that meeting really well, Mike. Have you been on a training course or something?" The praise was meant to be genuine but ended up by implying that people were surprised Mike had the ability to run the meeting that well. This is insulting and somewhat confusing for Mike. Alternatively, people praising others often put themselves down ("That's a good piece of typing, I wish I could do that well"), they are mealymouthed ("I hope it doesn't offend you if I say you did well there"), or they only use praise manipulatively, e.g., to get people to do more work for them.

The basic problem with giving praise is that there is an underlying feeling that it is somehow a sign of weakness on your part. It is not. It is honest, it is fair, and it is highly motivational.

In order to give praise effectively, consider the following rules.

- Be specific. Don't just say, "I liked the presentation of that document" but add specific reasons why: "Your use of highlighting and shading really makes the important point stand out clearly."
- Personalize. Use people's names when praising them so that they know you are directing your praise to them specifically.
- Avoid padding. This often sounds insincere and gushing.
- Be clear it is your praise you are giving. Do not reduce the effect of giving praise by saying, "The company will approve of this" or using similar phrases that depersonalize the praise. Make it very clear that you are impressed and you are giving the praise.

Throughout the dialogue, maintain an assertive tone of voice and body language.

Receiving Praise

If we lack practice at giving praise then, consequently, we almost certainly lack practice at receiving it. The "stiff upper lip" often leads us to feel almost guilty when receiving praise and we reduce the impact with statements like "It was nothing really, I was only doing my job." This has the effect of throwing praise back impolitely at the person offering it. Start from the assumption that it is not impolite or reason for guilt to agree with praise.

Another reason we try to reduce the effect of praise is that it is so often used manipulatively that we fear we are about to be placed under an obligation to do more work, more overtime, and so on. Start from the position that accepting praise places you under no obligations.

Rules for accepting praise

- Respond briefly, honestly, and personally, e.g., "Thank you, Susan. I am glad you liked the report."
- If you agree with the praise do not be afraid to say so, e.g., "Thank you. I was pleased with the report myself."
- If you disagree with the praise do not argue with the person giving it, because that would be very rude if the praise is given genuinely. Even if you disagree with it, it is still polite to thank the person giving it.

Assertively Making and Refusing Requests

We all have to make requests for resources, help, and so on virtually every working day. Given that amount of practice, it is astonishing just how badly it is often done.

Rules for making requests

Keep it brief and to the point

If your request is appropriate, then you do not have to justify it, apologize for it, or explain it extensively. Make a brief, specific request that sets out precisely what you require. Resist the temptation to drop hints; these are usually vague, unclear, and lacking in commitment. Give reasons if appropriate.

Although you do not have to make excuses or give apologies for your request, it may be more useful for the person you are making the request of if you supply him with some information as to why he should comply. Honest reasons offered also demonstrate the openness of your request.

Remember that a request is not a command

If your request is genuine, then the person you are making the request of has the option of saying yes or no. Make sure that you respect the right of the other person to say no in appropriate situations and do not be offended by a refusal. If you demonstrate that you are offended, the person you are speaking to might feel guilty and comply when she does not feel it appropriate; you will have set up the beginnings of a barrier to constructive assertive dialogue.

Rules for refusing requests

As is stated above, if a request is being made, then there is an implication of compliance or refusal with that request. If you feel that you are correct in refusing a request, then do so assertively as follows.

Do not be manipulated

You should not start from the presumption that it is rude to make a refusal, that you have no rights in the matter, or that you will offend others. If you are offending others by legitimately refusing a request, then the fault is in them and not you, because they are failing to respect your rights to refuse. There is no need to apologize for refusing appropriately.

Be brief

Make your refusal brief and clear but do not be abrupt. Make your statements straightforward: "I would rather not . . ." and so on.

Do not make excuses

The main reason not to make an excuse, apart from the fact that it is nonassertive, is that it will probably backfire. If someone asks you to stay late at work tonight and you reply, "I would like to but I am going out tonight," then you are highly likely to be met with the response, "That's fine. Then perhaps you can stay late tomorrow." Your reply gave permission for that response because you indicated that you are happy to stay late at some time (which in fact you may not be). If you then want to get out of it tomorrow, you have to come up with another excuse and they will get increasingly thin very quickly. Eventually you will back yourself into having to do what you do not want to do.

Personalize

When refusing a request, use the person's name. "I am grateful, Joan, but I would rather not." People will often feel comfortable hiding behind the facade of their company, making requests on behalf of this impersonal corporation. When you use their name and bring them out from behind the facade, they will be less comfortable pursuing improper requests in their own name.

You may be undecided as to whether you want to comply or say no to a request. There is nothing improper about asking for more information so that you can make a proper decision. Take the situation where someone comes to your desk and says, "Would you mind typing just a few letters for me?" You might assess what seems to be the situation and determine that a few letters could be typed in 20 minutes or so and you agree. Then the person brings you 60 letters to be typed or three letters each of 100 pages. At that point, you realize you have just committed yourself to a day's work and you begin to back out of it. The person who has made the request then manipulates you further (and be in no doubt that his or her initial request was made in a way intended to manipulate you) by trying to make you feel guilty, e.g., "Oh, when you told me you would, I confirmed to our suppliers that they would have the letters in the mail tonight. Now you are making me look a fool."

In situations where there is possible ambiguity, you have every right to ask for all the information you need in order to make a proper decision, e.g., "How many is a few?" or "How many pages in total would that be?" You might specify your own boundaries, e.g., "I am very busy at the moment, but I could certainly give you half an hour if that would help." By specifying your limitations, you have paved the way to challenge any improper manipulation. As a response to the last phrase, the person might say "Oh, I am sure you could do it in half an hour" and then give you several hours of work. You have every right to point out immediately, "No, this will take several hours and that is beyond the commitment I made to you. I can still offer you the half hour but at that time I must return the work to you in whatever state it is and leave it to you to make further arrangements, or you might like to make alternative arrangements immediately."

Although it is true that, for example, someone who cannot type may not estimate easily how long typing takes, in the vast majority of these situations you know, and they know, that they were disguising the truth in order to manipulate it and you should not feel guilty about challenging that very openly.

Giving and Receiving Criticism

Rules for giving constructive criticism

We all at some time have to give criticism. If we feel embarrassed or guilty then we will act in a nonassertive manner, which will usually not persuade the person to whom we are speaking to change his or her ways. If we feel angry, then we will act in an aggressive manner, which often worsens relationships rather than improves them. It is important that we comply with assertive rules for giving criticism as follows.

Have an objective in mind

Before giving criticism, ask yourself why you are doing it and what you want to achieve by it. If your only objective is to let off steam because something has made you angry, then you will be aggressive, you will not agree on a change that will make you less angry in the future, and you will create a barrier between yourself and the person you are speaking to. The objective of most criticism must be to make sure that whatever was wrong does not arise again or that mistakes that are made can be used as a learning process for future success. Whatever the objective, be sure that it is clear in your mind.

Introduce the boundaries of the criticism

When you first begin speaking to the person to whom you have to give criticism, she will be facing the unknown. The unknown is always a greater fear than the known. She will be concerned at how wide or how serious the criticism is; she may even be unsure of the area of the criticism if she has a few skeletons locked in her closet. This can make her defensive and she could become either nonassertive or aggressive very quickly. By immediately setting out the specific area of the criticism, you reduce the tension and the need for defensive posturing.

Be specific

As with all assertiveness rules, make sure that you are specific about the criticism you are making. Do not, for example, say, "There have been a lot of mistakes in the typing lately," but rather "In the past week, I have noticed six serious errors in letters you have prepared."

If you are vague, then you leave room for the person to defend himself on the basis that you are misperceiving the situation or that you are being unfair. When you make a quantifiable statement of fact, a lot of unnecessary posturing can be gotten out of the way very quickly, as the person can only agree or ask you to support your statement (which you should then be able to do, having prepared yourself for the meeting with the appropriate proof).

Do not personalize

Just as it is highly motivational to personalize a statement of praise, so it reduces the demotivational effect of criticism if you depersonalize statements. Depersonalized statements also address the work-related problem rather than the individual. For example, do not say, "You are getting careless with your typing lately," but rather say, "There have been a number of mistakes in your typing lately." The mistakes are a fact; her carelessness is an opinion, which again can lead to unnecessary posturing.

Get a response

When you have set out the problem as you see it, make sure that you get a response from the person you are speaking to, with questions like "Do you agree?," "Why do you think this is happening?," and so on.

There are various reasons for insisting on a response at this stage. First, the person you are speaking to may be feeling defensive and feel that you are attacking her. When you get into dialogue with her, she will more quickly become part of the solution rather than having it imposed on her. Second, you want to be sure that she is going to approach your criticism constructively rather than hear you out and then storm off in a mood. The response you get will dictate your next action: if it is constructive, then begin to build a solution for the future; if it is aggressive or nonassertive, then follow the rules given for dealing with nonassertive or aggressive people above.

The response should be verbal and not merely a nod of the head or body language acknowledgment. It is very important, if you are to build constructive solutions, that any "ice" between you is broken. Those of you who have been in training rooms will recognize a simple technique used by trainers to break the ice early in the day. One of the first things they will do is ask everyone to introduce themselves to the group. Although the information given in that introduction is often useful for the trainer, highlighting individual issues, and so on, one of the main reasons is to get people to hear their own voices in the acoustics of that room and in that group so that they will not be embarrassed to speak up during the day. This leads to a more dynamic creative atmosphere with everyone feeling she has input. This is the atmosphere that you want for your constructive solution building. Imagine a situation where you have gone into a training room where all the delegates and the trainer have been freely speaking throughout the day. It is now 3 o'clock in the afternoon and you have not said a word. You will find it very difficult to make your first contribution and indeed you will probably avoid doing so. The same happens in the dialogue of criticism giving. If the person you are speaking to does not enter into that dialogue very quickly, then in a short time a barrier builds up that makes it increasingly difficult for her to contribute. You must force that contribution as early as possible in order to get into a mutually beneficial constructive dynamic atmosphere.

Ask for feedback

Once you have reached a situation of constructive dialogue (i.e., you have got through any nonassertive or aggressive behavior), do not impose changes. When you impose changes on the person you are speaking to, then if he fails to meet those changes, he can always come back and say, "Well, it was never a reasonable request you were making but I didn't think you were giving me any choice but to try." In other words he has a ready-made excuse for failure. If you ask him for feedback and suggestions as to what can be done and if you build a solution with him, it will be a solution to which he is committed, both morally and practically.

Summarize the meeting

As with all assertiveness, a firm and clear commitment must be made. Once you have agreed to the changes with the person, then make a commitment to review the position to make sure that those changes have been implemented. For example, you might say, "We will have another meeting in a month's time and review your typing. If the changes we have agreed on are effective, then there should be no further difficulties and I will expect that to be the case."

It is not reasonable to ask people to make a goal of an indefinite requirement. Obviously we want the typing to be to a good standard indefinitely, but we cannot leave the sword of Damocles hanging over the typist's head on the basis that there is no time at which she can prove she has mended her ways. If there is a deadline for review, she has to meet a certain standard for a certain time period, and when you have that review you can either comment on a failure to meet the commitment with discrepancy assertion or give open and honest praise. Have that review whatever the outcome, and do make sure that you make it clear that what has now been achieved is to be carried on into the future. Combine that requirement with the praise you are giving.

The logic is that, having found a way to correct previous errors and produce quality work, people will get into that new habit and continuing quality will become a matter of routine rather than effort.

Rules for receiving criticism

If we must learn to give criticism constructively, then we must also learn to receive it constructively. Indeed, anyone learning how to give or receive criticism should learn the rules for both sides of the coin, so that constructive dialogue is mutual.

Consider the rights of others

Although criticism always feels like an attack and we always feel disappointed in ourselves to be criticized, we have to acknowledge that other people have a right to criticize if we have failed to meet commitments or work to a standard they know we can achieve. Start, then, by knowing that criticism is not of itself unfair or improper. Remember too that people may not be skilled at giving criticism and may come over aggressively or nonassertively; the fact that it may be your boss or that you may be on the receiving end should not prevent you from acting assertively and seeking to deal with her in a way that makes her more assertive and less aggressive or nonassertive.

Make sure that criticism is specific

Just as we have made clear that criticism given should be specific rather than vague and should address the work problem rather than the personality, so you have the right to question any vagueness in order that the person justifies his comments with specifics. Furthermore, if you feel that you are personally being criticized in an improper way, then you have a right not to be. For example, if someone were to say "You are basically a very lazy person, aren't you?" that (even if it happened to be true!) would be an inappropriate way to criticize constructively. Your best assertive response is to address the specific work-related problems and pointedly not to respond to personalized statements.

Clarify future outcomes

It is in your interest to clarify what future outcomes are expected of you so that you can measure your success or defend any further criticism that might be improperly directed at you.

Disagree if appropriate

If you believe the criticism is incorrect or unfair, then you have the right to say so. You will make the greatest impact if you can offer examples in your defense. Remember, however, that you will not be able to disagree with facts presented to you, only the context in which those facts are presented; if, for example, you felt that one or two mistakes being pointed out to you were unreasonable in the light of the amount of work you were doing. However, do not get into a numbers war; if the person speaking to you produces evidence of six mistyped letters, do not triumphantly pull out of your briefcase three that you did correctly!

Nonverbal attitude

As with all interactive exchanges, make sure that you maintain assertive eye contact, open body language, and an appropriate facial expression.

Making Interruptions

Most secretaries have to learn how to interrupt their bosses' meetings or appointments at some time. There are certain practical rules to consider.

Be sure the interruption is necessary and welcomed

You will have to make your own judgments on whether the interruptions are necessary, and no doubt you will learn by experience (nobody ever learned to ride a bike without bruising their knees and elbows). A few commonsense rules can be applied. First, make sure that urgency is a factor; otherwise deliver the message when the meeting is over. Second, make sure that there is no one else who can appropriately deal with the situation, at least for the time being. Third, discuss interruptions with your boss and as part of your boss–secretary partnership solicit his opinions as to what he thinks is an appropriate interruption.

Write down the message and have it with you in case verbal interruption is impossible or difficult

Even though you may be intending to use the appropriate methods to interrupt your boss verbally in a meeting (see below), it may be impossible. When you arrive in the room, you may find that she is in the middle of a long presentation that should not be interrupted. If you have the message written down, you can deal with this situation. You go to the place where your boss is sitting (even if she is now standing delivering a presentation), place the message clearly and squarely in the middle of her desk or the area she is using on the table, and make eye contact with her to make sure that she knows you have delivered the message. The eye contact alone will indicate the urgency of the message, the fact of its delivery, and your reasonableness in not having interrupted her. The responsibility to act sensibly from this point on is now laid at your boss's door.

In the majority of situations, you will be able to interrupt verbally, in which case the following rules apply.

Hover briefly

Hovering is an important skill in assertive interruption, which so easily goes wrong. When you are going to interrupt a person who may be talking or who may be listening to someone else talking, you should walk up close to her and then pause for a brief time before making the interruption. This gives the person time to become aware that you are there and to get into a frame of mind to respond appropriately to you. This hovering should last for approximately four seconds. Then, whether you have been acknowledged or not, you have the right to begin to deliver the message. Not hovering is the equivalent of barging in unannounced and uninvited, and is rude. If you hover for very much more than four seconds, certainly more than ten, you begin to get locked into a cycle where you cannot speak until you are verbally invited to do so. People concentrating on others, people unaware of your being there, or blatantly rude people may leave you standing for several minutes before they acknowledge you. You should not have to put up with that rudeness but in this instance you will have caused it yourself. It is also not particularly pleasant for others in the group, who will inadvertently be watching one of the less savory traits of the person you are attempting to interrupt as she rudely ignores your appropriate interruption.

Be polite but firm

Even if it is part of your relationship with your boss to refer to him by his first name, it is probably more appropriate to address him more formally when interrupting him in a meeting. Deliver the message concisely and factually and ask if there is anything you can do to help, e.g., deliver an interim response or get some information ready.

Never whisper or take someone away from a group without explanation

In any given group, there are usually paranoid and/or mischievous people. If, particularly in a male–female situation, you walk into a room and quietly whisper into the ear of your boss, who then gets up and leaves with you, there will be those around the table who feel that it is something adverse to do with them and those who will take the opportunity of "rib digging" humor. This does not mean that you have to discuss your boss's confidential matters publicly. You might, for example, say, "Excuse me, I must have a word with Ms. Jones outside as we have just received an urgent message for her." This makes clear the nature of the interruption without specifying the possibly confidential details.

Exiting from a Situation

Secretaries are rather prone to getting caught at office parties by the office bore. Unfortunately this often relates to the improper perception of secretaries as menial and reflects the fact that the vast majority of secretaries are women and that the office bore is usually a man. Being nonassertive or aggressive, and therefore having problems in his relationships with other staff, he picks up someone he feels he can dominate and bores in. There are specific rules for exiting from situations when you feel that the time has come to end a conversation.

Announce a time for exiting

Try not to be vague about your plans to leave without being overly precise. For example, you might say, "I must leave in five minutes." Do not say, "I have to leave shortly," because shortly is a long time to the office bore, and do not be ridiculously precise: "I can give you another 45 seconds."

Use the five minutes

During the five-minute period that you have announced, retract from the situation in terms of eye contact, body language, and verbal cues, i.e., reduce your eye contact, stop saying yes or no to statements being offered, reduce your enthusiastic nodding or shaking of the head, and very gradually back slightly away from the person.

Interrupting

At about the five-minute point or at any appropriate time, listen for natural pauses in the other person's speaking (even bores have to breathe sometimes!) and interrupt verbally and nonverbally. Put a hand on the person's arm and make a clear statement ("I must leave now"). This makes it difficult for all but the most persistent bore to continue. If there is persistence, then move your hand from his arm and make a gesture between a wave and a blocking gesture, effectively putting the outstretched palm of your hand between your two faces. This makes conversation virtually impossible and makes your exit almost certain.

Be persistent

Despite the persistence of others, you have a right to persistence too and no matter what protestations are made you should now back away from the exchange firmly and promptly.

Never make excuses

If you do not want to continue with the conversation, say so politely but firmly. Do not make excuses like "We can discuss this later." The office bore will go and get a drink and spend the rest of the evening watching for the moment when you are free from other conversation and will then take up your offer and begin to discuss the matter again. Excuses include false interruptions. One person we spoke to always made arrangements with a fellow secretary that if she gave a particular signal, the other secretary was to come across and say that a fax for the first secretary had just been received and take her away from the situation. Although this has an immediate effect, it creates several problems. First, people begin to wonder why the company is receiving so many faxes at such bizarre times. Second, you feel bad for taking the coward's way out. And third, you have to come out of the bathroom at some time, and when you do you will be pounced on to continue the conversation!

Is Assertiveness Always Right?

In the vast majority of interactive situations at work or in everyday life, assertiveness is the only proper response or behavior pattern. However, there are always going to be extreme circumstances where assertiveness is not always right.

Violent angry people and those under the influence of alcohol or drugs do not always respond to assertiveness. It is outside the scope of this book to consider appropriate responses to such people, but we will note that a wider range of possibilities than assertive dialogue and behavior may be necessary.

There might be compassionate reasons. For example, if a blind person pushed in front of you in a line, you might not feel it appropriate to challenge him. However, if you felt that the person was taking advantage of you, possibly using his blindness, then there is no reason why you should not assert yourself. Disability does not give a person more rights than you and, indeed, to offer more rights to disabled people is itself insulting.

Aggression can sometimes be expedient. For example, if you have to clear out a building because there is a fire, it is hardly appropriate to gather people into a group and assertively try to enlighten them as to the benefits of leaving the building. Grab them by the hands and arms, push them toward doors, speak clearly, and accept no interruptions or arguments. When everyone is safely outside, you can apologize for your brusqueness, which of course they will understand.

A Sense of Humor

You might have noticed that throughout our discussion of assertiveness, there has been no reference to using humor. The examples are serious sounding, even dour. This is not to say that humor should not be part of business life; indeed, it is extremely important. However, inappropriate delivery of humor can cause great difficulty and misunderstanding. We have therefore not attempted to suggest styles of humor and we leave this to the individual to determine. However, in determining an appropriate level of humor, or an appropriate time to use or not use humor, all of the rules of assertiveness, nonassertiveness, and aggression that we have covered in this section apply. By all means use humor to oil the wheels of communication, but not for sarcasm, put-downs, belittlement, self-aggrandizement, and so on.

Starting Out

Now that you understand what assertiveness is and how it works, and you have many practical examples of how to begin to apply it, you should consider when you are first going to try your hand at it. As a rule, don't try to climb up Everest before you have walked up Snowdon. If, for example, you are going to learn to interrupt, you might first start at dinner parties in your own house with friends or, if you want to try it on your boss, at times when it is not crucial to her. The place not to try your first interruption is in the middle of a an uneasy shareholders' meeting!

When you are setting commitments, make them reasonably obtainable so that you first get to feel the benefit of success before you set the commitments that will stretch you.

Set aside a half hour one evening a week to review your week. Review the times when you acted most assertively and analyze how you did it, why you did it, and what the outcomes were. Also review the times when you acted nonassertively or aggressively, and again study why you did it and what the outcomes were. In those cases, also consider how you should have behaved assertively.

Make plans ahead. You cannot of course predict situations ahead in detail any more than you can prepare ad-lib jokes ahead of time, but you can predict certain situations that are likely to arise and in which you are more than likely to have to act, in one way or another. Think ahead to those times, think through how you plan to act, and try to act accordingly. For example, if you know that you are going to be the minutes secretary at certain meetings, you will probably know most of the personalities who will be at the meeting and you can think through responses that you are likely to have to give to certain areas (particularly if you know what is being discussed if you prepared the agenda).

Make assertiveness a habit and a routine and not something that you do for three weeks and then forget about. Several of the processes and suggestions we have given can continue for the rest of your life: your commitments on index cards, your weekly review of yourself, and so on.

We will break our own rules and indulge in one—appropriate—cliché to remind you when to start your assertive behavior: *tomorrow is the first day of the rest of your life.*

Index

NOTES

NOTES